Letts

KS1 Success

Age 5-7

Science

Revision & Practice

Jill Atkins

Revision Guide

Plants

Seasonal Changes

Animals, Including Humans

Living Things and their Habitats

Everyday Materials

Workbook

Flowers

Wild flowers are found mainly in the countryside. If they are in the garden, they are often called weeds.

Here are some wild flowers you might know.

primrose   bluebell   dandelion   daisy   clover   violet   poppy   foxglove

Cultivated flowers are mainly grown in gardens. Sometimes you might find them in the countryside.

Here are some garden flowers you might know.

daffodil   crocus   tulip   sunflower   sweet pea   rose   pansy

Fruit and vegetable plants

Fruit and vegetables are grown on farms and in market gardens. When they are **ripe**, they are taken to shops for people to buy. Fruit and vegetables are grown all over the world. They are brought to our country by ship or plane.

Some people grow fruit and vegetables in their gardens or on allotments.

We often think of pumpkins, courgettes, tomatoes, peppers and cucumbers as vegetables. They are really fruit because they contain seeds to grow into more plants.

pumpkin   courgette   tomato   pepper   cucumber

Trees

Many trees and plants are **deciduous**. Their leaves die and drop off in the autumn. For example:

| oak | beech | pear | apple | silver birch | horse chestnut |

Other trees are **evergreen**. They have leaves all the year round. For example:

| cedar | fir | pine | holly | ivy | laurel |

Trees have different-shaped leaves. Some evergreen trees have needles. Others have dark green shiny leaves.

| oak | beech | horse chestnut | holly | pine needles |

Listen up
1

Parent tip! Some wild flowers are rare, so remind your child not to pick them.

Keywords

Wild ➤ Plants that grow naturally without human help

Cultivated ➤ Plants that are grown and cared for

Ripe ➤ Fruit and vegetables that are fully developed and ready for harvesting and eating

Deciduous ➤ A tree or plant that sheds its leaves in autumn every year

Evergreen ➤ A tree that has leaves all year round

Have a go!
Go for a walk and look for wild flowers. See if you can spot some deciduous and evergreen trees. Collect leaves of different shapes and make leaf prints.

Draw some fruit, vegetables, flowers or trees.

Test yourself

❶ Circle the two deciduous trees. Underline the two evergreen trees.

cedar   oak   beech   pine

❷ What do you call plants that are grown and cared for?

❸ Why is a cucumber a fruit, not a vegetable?

❹ Name three wild flowers.

Flowers

Many flowers grow from a **seed**. Seeds grow into flowers of different colours, shapes and sizes. In gardens, people sow seeds where they want plants to grow. Wild flowers scatter their seeds in autumn and plants grow from the seeds in spring.

Here are some interesting facts about seeds.

- Foxglove seeds are tiny.
- Dandelion seeds are sometimes called a 'dandelion clock'. Have you ever picked one and blown it, scattering the seeds into the wind?
- A sunflower seed can grow into a plant of 3 metres or more. Birds and pets feed on sunflower seeds. You can eat roasted sunflower seeds, too!

Some flowers grow from a **bulb**. For example:

| daffodil | tulip | crocus | hyacinth |

Flowers are sometimes called blossom, especially when they are on a bush or tree. For example: apple blossom   hawthorn

Look at the flower that has grown from a seed (daisy). How does it differ from the flower that has grown from a bulb (daffodil)?

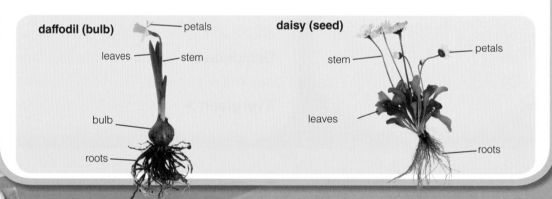

daffodil (bulb) — petals, leaves, stem, bulb, roots

daisy (seed) — petals, stem, leaves, roots

Fruit and vegetables

Fruit is the part of the plant that holds the seed. For example, if you cut open an apple, the pips are inside.

Vegetables are from different parts of the plant. For example:

- carrots and parsnips are the **root**
- cabbage, lettuce and spinach are the **leaves**
- broccoli and cauliflower are the **flower**.

Listen up 2

Trees

Here is a diagram of an apple tree.

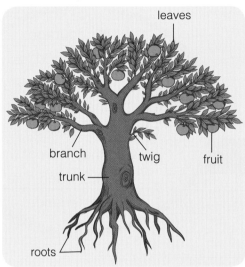

Tree trunks and branches are protected by **bark**. Each type of tree has a different texture and pattern of bark.

Top tip!

Touch and feel the bark of different types of trees. Can you notice the different textures? Hold a large sheet of paper on the bark of each tree and rub the paper with the side of a wax crayon. You will get a different texture pattern for each type of tree.

Working scientifically

Bulb experiment

What you need

- a hyacinth bulb
- a glass jar with the opening at the top a bit smaller than the bulb (you can buy specially shaped jars)
- cold water

What to do

1 Half-fill the jar with water.

2 Place the bulb on top of the jar.

3 Put the bulb in a dark cupboard. Check it every few days.

4 When roots grow towards the water and a small shoot appears from the centre of the bulb, take the bulb out of the cupboard.

5 Watch the roots grow longer and the shoots grow upwards.

6 After about 14 weeks, a flower will grow. What colour do you think it will be?

7 Record what you see in a chart.

Have a go! Use a magnifying glass to study a flower. Make a list or draw what you can see.

Test yourself

1 Name three flowers grown from a bulb.

2 Which part of a plant holds the seed?

3 What is a dandelion clock?

4 Why do trees have bark?

All plants need **water**, **warmth** and **light** to grow strong.

If plants do not have enough water, they **wilt** and die. They get most of their water through their roots, then up through the stem. It is like drinking through a straw!

Seeds and bulbs do not need light. Over winter, they stay **dormant** underground or in packets.

Parent tip! Encourage your child to join in as many nature activities as possible so that they learn through first-hand experience.

Bulbs

How does a bulb grow?

1 When the bulb feels warmth from the Sun and moisture from the rain, roots begin to grow from the base of the bulb.

2 Green leaves begin to grow inside.

3 They push up through the soil into the light.

4 Leaves grow longer and a shoot grows in the centre of the plant.

5 The shoot grows longer and becomes a stem.

6 A bud grows on the stem.

7 This bud becomes the flower.

Some vegetables are bulbs.

leek   garlic   onion

Seeds

Seeds also store food for the plant that will grow from them. When they feel warmth and moisture, they send out roots and shoots and begin to grow.

The picture shows the life cycle of a plant.

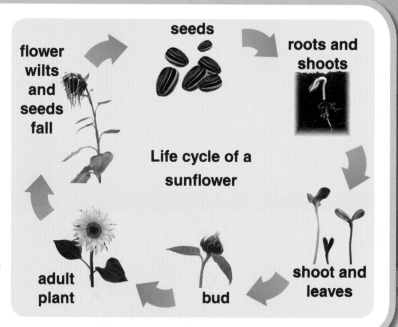

flower wilts and seeds fall

seeds

roots and shoots

Life cycle of a sunflower

shoot and leaves

bud

adult plant

Trees

Trees are plants. Trees grow from seeds. The seeds have different names. For example:

- an **oak tree** grows from an **acorn**
- a **pear tree** grows from a **pear pip**
- a **peach tree** grows from a **peach stone**
- a **horse chestnut tree** grows from a **conker**
- a **pine tree** grows from **pine nuts** that grow inside **pine cones**.

Some trees have roots that stretch as wide and deep underground as the branches do above ground.

Working scientifically

Seed experiment

1. Put some soil into two trays. Plant sunflower seeds in both of them.
2. Put both trays in a warm place.
3. Water one tray but don't water the other one.
4. Look at the trays every day.
5. Do both sets of seeds grow? If not, why do you think that is?

Keywords

Wilt ➤ Become limp and droop, often turning yellow and then brown

Dormant ➤ Asleep and ready to be active when the time is right

Listen up 3

Have a go!

Collect seeds from fruit in your home and from outside. Examples include apple and orange pips, melon seeds, peach stones, conkers, acorns and beech nuts.
Draw and label the seeds. Order them from smallest to largest.

Test yourself

1. What is the seed of an oak tree called?
2. What three things do plants need to grow?
3. How do plants get moisture?
4. What does dormant mean?

This mind map will help you remember all the main points from this topic. Have a go at drawing your own mind map.

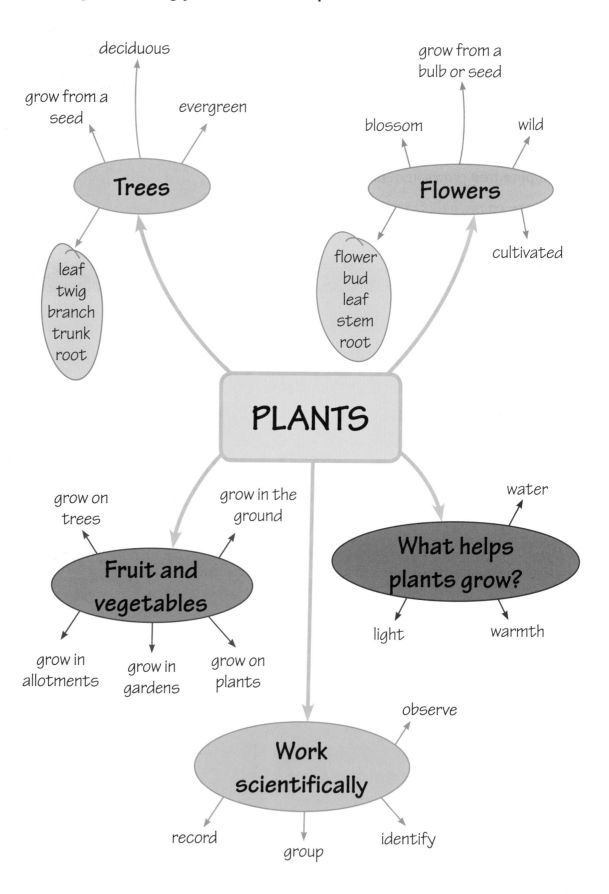

1 Fill in the gaps using these words.

conker   **seed in a stone**   **pip**   **pine nut**   **acorn**

a. An oak tree grows from an .... **(1 mark)**

b. A pear tree grows from a .... **(1 mark)**

c. A pine tree grows from a .... **(1 mark)**

d. A horse chestnut tree grows from a .... **(1 mark)**

e. A peach tree grows from a .... **(1 mark)**

2 Which part of a plant acts like a drinking straw?   **(1 mark)**

....

3 Name an evergreen plant that has prickly leaves.   **(1 mark)**

....

4 What do you call flowers that grow on bushes and hedges?   **(1 mark)**

....

5 Name three vegetables that are bulbs.   **(3 marks)**

....

6 Which part of a bulb grows first?   **(1 mark)**

....

7 Write the parts of the plant in the correct places using
these words.   **(5 marks)**

stem   **roots**   **leaf**   **flower**   **petal**

The seasons

There are **four seasons** each year: **spring**, **summer**, **autumn** and **winter**. The world goes through many changes as the seasons change. Those changes make a difference to the lives of humans and other living things.

Spring

In spring, the weather slowly becomes warmer.
The days get longer and plants begin to come to life.

During spring:

- different flowers appear, such as snowdrops, primroses and crocuses (the snowdrop is usually the first flower to appear)
- catkins hang from hazel trees
- leaves sprout from buds on trees and bushes
- birds make nests, lay eggs and their chicks hatch
- hedgehogs wake up from **hibernation** and look for food
- frogs, toads and newts wake up and return to their pond to lay eggs (spawn).

Summer

Listen up
4

In summer, the days are long and the nights are short. The weather is at its warmest and the Sun is at its highest in the sky. People wear light clothing and children play outside.

During summer:

- plants flower and give fruit
- trees are full of leaves and give shade from the Sun
- many birds, such as swallows, **migrate** here from other countries
- animals and birds can find plenty of food to eat
- there are lots of butterflies, ladybirds, bees and other insects.

Parent tip! Make sure your child knows that they must never look directly at the Sun, even through sunglasses. The Sun can burn the retina at the back of the eye.

Autumn

In autumn, the days get shorter. The weather is cooler and people need to heat their houses and wear more clothes.

During autumn:
- flowers die and develop seeds
- some plants die
- leaves of deciduous trees change colour and fall to the ground
- some birds **migrate** to warmer countries
- animals and birds eat as much as they can before the winter comes
- frogs, toads and newts leave their ponds and look for a sheltered place, such as under a log, to sleep.

Keywords

Hibernate ➤ A deep sleep which some animals fall into during winter

Migrate ➤ Birds fly long distances from one country to another, according to the seasons

Winter

In winter, the days are short and the nights are long. It gets dark in the middle of the afternoon. People wear warm clothes, such as hats, gloves and scarves. Sometimes it is cold enough for snow!

During winter:
- seeds and bulbs lie under the ground, waiting for the warmer weather
- deciduous trees have bare branches; evergreen trees stay green
- many people feed robins, blackbirds and other birds that take shelter in bushes on colder days
- animals like hedgehogs **hibernate** because there is less food for them to eat
- frogs, toads and newts **hibernate** too
- animals such as the badger and rabbit do not hibernate but they stay in their underground homes most of the time and sleep a lot because it is warmer there.

Make a weather chart that shows rain, sunshine, cloud, snow and wind.

For each type of weather, write or draw what you would wear.

1 Put the seasons in the right order, starting with spring.

winter   summer   spring   autumn

2 In which season do hedgehogs hibernate?

3 In which season do leaves change colour and fall to the ground?

4 In which season are the days shortest?

The weather

The weather affects all living things.

Listen up 5

The Sun

Most people love the Sun. It gives plants, animals and humans light and warmth.

The Sun is in the sky every day. If the weather is cloudy, the Sun is hidden and the day is dull.

In the desert, the Sun is extremely hot. There is very little rain, so most plants cannot grow.

Top tip! To help keep healthy bones, go out in sunlight as much as you can. You need to protect your skin from the Sun, so always apply sunscreen.

Clouds

Clouds are made of water droplets. Sometimes these droplets fall to Earth as rain, sleet, hail or snow.

If clouds build up and become dark and heavy, there may be a storm with thunder and lightning.

Rain

Rain can fall in any season. When rain falls, some of it is stored in **reservoirs**, man-made large lakes, where it is kept until humans need it.

Rain is very important for plants, animals and humans.

- Plants need rain to help them grow.
- Animals and birds need rain to drink.
- Humans need water for drinking, washing hands, bathing, washing clothes and farming.

Here are some more facts about rain.

- Sometimes there is too much rain. This can cause **floods**.
- If there is no rain for a long time, there is a **drought**.
- When the Sun shines, but there is a rain shower at the same time, a rainbow appears.

Wind

Sometimes the air is still, but often the wind blows. The coldest wind usually comes from the north, but can come from the east as well.

Here are some interesting facts about wind.
- The wind blows seeds. Where they land is where they will grow.
- Wind is useful for things like drying washing and for keeping the air fresh, and you can have fun flying a kite when it is windy!
- If the wind is too strong, like a **hurricane**, it can cause a lot of damage.

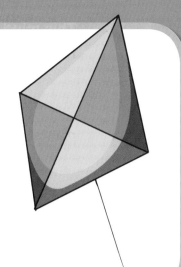

Sleet, hail and snow

Sleet, hail and snow fall in colder weather.
- **Sleet** is rain containing some ice or snowflakes.
- **Hail** is pieces of frozen rain.
- **Snow** is water that is frozen into ice crystals. They fall as white flakes. Each snowflake is made up of many crystals of ice. Each tiny crystal is shaped like a six-pointed star. Each one is different.

Keywords

Reservoir ➤ A lake specially made for storing water

Flood ➤ When there is too much water in a short time. River banks burst and water runs over the land and sometimes floods buildings

Drought ➤ When there is no rain for a long time. The ground dries, plants die, and animals and humans do not have enough water

Hurricane ➤ A very, very strong wind that blows down trees and damages buildings

Working scientifically

When it snows, look at snowflakes through a magnifying glass. You will need to be very quick or the snowflake will melt! Try to draw some of the patterns you see.

Make pretty snowflake shapes from folded circles of white paper.

Have a go!

Test yourself

❶ How many points does a snowflake crystal have?

❷ Name four ways we use water.

❸ What are clouds made of?

❹ What two things does the Sun give to plants, animals and humans?

This mind map will help you remember all the main points from this topic. Have a go at drawing your own mind map.

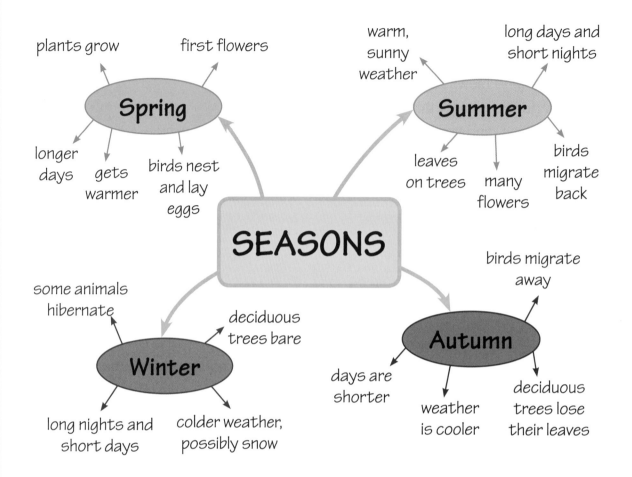

plants grow

first flowers

warm, sunny weather

long days and short nights

Spring

Summer

longer days

gets warmer

birds nest and lay eggs

leaves on trees

many flowers

birds migrate back

SEASONS

some animals hibernate

deciduous trees bare

birds migrate away

Winter

Autumn

days are shorter

long nights and short days

colder weather, possibly snow

weather is cooler

deciduous trees lose their leaves

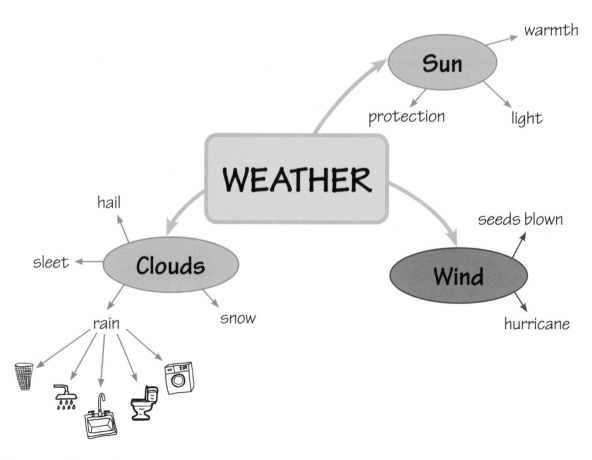

warmth

Sun

protection

light

WEATHER

hail

seeds blown

sleet

Clouds

Wind

rain

snow

hurricane

1 Fill in the gaps with one of the seasons.

> spring   summer   autumn   winter

a. Birds build nests in ....   **(1 mark)**

b. Deciduous trees have bare branches in ....   **(1 mark)**

c. The days are longest in ....   **(1 mark)**

d. Primroses and crocuses appear in ....   **(1 mark)**

e. There is less food for birds and animals in ....   **(1 mark)**

f. Leaves change colour and fall in ....   **(1 mark)**

2 Circle three animals that hibernate.

frog   cat   mouse   hedgehog   robin   toad   rabbit   **(3 marks)**

3 Why do some animals, such as hedgehogs, hibernate?   **(2 marks)**

....

....

4 Why do people wear more clothes in winter?   **(2 marks)**

....

5 Why do frogs return to their ponds in spring?   **(1 mark)**

....

6 What is the first flower to usually appear in spring?   **(1 mark)**

....

7 Why must you never look directly at the Sun?   **(1 mark)**

....

8 Tick (✓) the box next to the correct statement.   **(1 mark)**

Drought is when there has been too much rain. ☐

Drought is when there has been no rain for a long time. ☐

Animals, Including Humans

Common animals

There are different groups of animals:

- mammals
- amphibians
- birds
- fish
- reptiles

Mammals

Many **mammals** live in the **countryside**. For example:

mouse rat hedgehog squirrel fox rabbit badger mole bat deer

Have you seen any of these mammals?

There are **wild** mammals all over the world. For example:

lion   tiger   giraffe   leopard   gopher

raccoon   polar bear   zebra   elephant

Some mammals live in the **ocean**. For example:

whale   dolphin   porpoise   seal   walrus

Some whales are much bigger than an elephant.
The blue whale is the largest mammal in the world.

Some mammals live in rivers. For example: otter   water rat

Do you have a **pet**?

Some pet mammals are kept in cages. For example:

hamster   guinea pig   gerbil   rabbit

Other pet mammals include: cats   dogs   horses

Some **farm** animals are mammals. For example:

cow   pig   sheep
horse   goat

Humans are mammals, too!

Always wash your hands after you have handled animals, even your pets.

Parent tip!

Listen up 6

Keyword

Mammals ➤ Warm-blooded animals that give birth to babies and feed them with milk

Amphibians

Amphibians live in water and on land. They need to stay near water so their smooth skin does not dry out.

For example: frog toad newt

Birds

You can see birds in gardens or parks. For example:

robin pigeon blue tit blackbird

Birds can be:
- **huge** like the ostrich
- **tiny** like the wren
- **brightly coloured** like the parrot.

Some birds are **raptors**. For example:

eagle kestrel

Keyword

Raptor ➤ A bird that hunts for its food. It has a hooked bill and sharp talons. It is also called a bird of prey

Fish

Fish live in water.

Some fish live in the sea.

For example:

shark tuna cod herring haddock

Some fish live in rivers, lakes and ponds.

For example:

pike salmon trout minnow

Reptiles

Reptiles live more on land than in water. They have scaly skin which does not dry out.

For example:

snake lizard crocodile alligator turtle

The tortoise is a reptile but it lives only on land.

Have a go! Make a list of mammals, amphibians, reptiles, fish or birds.

How many different animals can you find?

Test yourself

❶ Name a reptile that lives only on land.

❷ What is the largest mammal in the world?

❸ Circle the five mammals.

whale mouse haddock
cow newt ostrich
gerbil salmon fox

All animals need food, but not all animals eat the same foods. They can be split into **carnivores**, **herbivores** and **omnivores**.

Listen up
7

Carnivores

Carnivores eat **only** the flesh of other animals. Many carnivores are predators.

Big cats (e.g. lions, tigers, leopards, pumas and lynx)

- hunt for other animals

leopard

Hawks and owls

- eat birds and small animals

hawk

Seals, sea lions, walruses, dolphins and porpoises

- eat fish

porpoise

Snakes and crocodiles (and other reptiles, apart from tortoises)

- eat other animals and birds

crocodile

Carnivore

Large fish (e.g. sharks)

- eat smaller fish and sea life

shark

Adult amphibians (e.g. frogs and toads)

- eat worms, flies and other insects

toad

Whales

Baleen whales

- no sharp teeth
- eat tiny sea creatures called plankton through their wide mouth, which has a kind of sieve across it

baleen whale

Killer whales

- also called orca
- have long, sharp teeth
- hunt and kill other whales, dolphins, seals and fish

killer whale

Herbivores

Herbivores eat **no** flesh of other animals. All of their food comes from plants.

- Humans that are herbivores are **vegetarian**. They do not eat meat or fish, but eat plenty of other food in a balanced and healthy diet.
- Other mammals that are herbivores include cows, sheep, deer, elephants, hippopotamuses, pandas, beavers, rabbits and mice.

Keywords

Predator ➤ A wild animal that hunts other animals for food
Vegetarian ➤ A person who does not eat meat or fish

Parent tip! Help your child find information about carnivores, herbivores and omnivores.

Omnivores

Omnivores eat a variety of food from both plants and animals. They are omnivorous.

Humans
- often eat meat, fish and food that comes from plants

Omnivore

Big dogs (including wolves and hyenas)
- hunt and kill other animals
- also eat fruit, nuts and berries

wolf

Bears
- eat fish and animals
- also eat berries, fruit and nuts

bear

Most birds
- eat insects and flies
- also eat seeds and berries

bird

Hedgehogs and rats
- eat vegetation
- also eat worms and insects

hedgehog

Have a go! Draw as many things as you can think of that an omnivorous person might eat.

Then tick everything that a vegetarian person would eat.

Test yourself

1 How do predators find their food?

2 Underline the four animals that are herbivores.

lion sheep elephant cat panda
bear rat beaver tiger

3 What does an omnivore eat?

Backbone

Many animals have a **backbone**, including mammals, birds, amphibians, reptiles and many fish. For example:

human monkey shark snake bird
whale cat frog crocodile wolf

The backbone is often called **the spine**. It stretches from the head to the end of the back and into the tail. The backbone is made up of bones called **vertebrae**.

Humans have a **skeleton**. Without a skeleton many animals, including humans, would be very floppy!

Many animals do not have a backbone. For example:

jellyfish worm crab bee butterfly
spider octopus shellfish

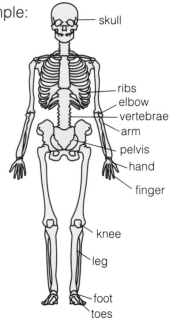

Human skeleton

- skull
- ribs
- elbow
- vertebrae
- arm
- pelvis
- hand
- finger
- knee
- leg
- foot
- toes

Top tip! Use your muscles by exercising to keep you fit and healthy.

Limbs

Most land animals with a backbone also have **limbs**. For example:

owl dog guinea pig rat giraffe elephant lizard human penguin

Humans can stand upright and walk on two feet. **Apes** and **monkeys** can also stand upright, but most of the time they move around on four legs.

Birds can stand upright and walk or hop on two feet. Their wings are limbs, too.

Some animals have a backbone, but no arms or legs. For example:

snake   dolphin   whale   shark

Fish, **whales**, **dolphins** and **sharks** have **fins** that guide them through the water. **Snakes** wriggle their bodies to help them move along the ground.

Animals and humans have **muscles** in their bodies, too.

How many limbs do these creatures below have? Can you see that the insects have **six legs** and the spider and octopus have **eight limbs**?

Teeth

Human babies are usually born without teeth. After a few months, teeth start to show.

How many teeth do you have? Your first set of teeth fall out when your adult teeth are ready to grow in their place. Adults grow 32 teeth altogether.

There are three different kinds of teeth because most humans are omnivores.
- **Incisors** are for cutting.
- **Canines** are for tearing.
- **Molars** are for chewing.

Cows and sheep have six strong molars, top and bottom, both sides, to help them chew grass.

Cats and dogs have long canines. These help them to tear food, such as other animals.

On the outside

The skeleton and muscles are on the inside, but what about the outside?

Different kinds of animals have different outsides. For example:
- tortoises, beetles and crabs have a hard shell
- whales and dolphins have smooth skin
- fish and snakes have scaly skin. As snakes grow they shed their skin. They have a new skin underneath.

Keywords

Vertebrae ➤ Small bones that form the backbone
Skeleton ➤ A framework of bones inside the body that supports the body of an animal
Limbs ➤ Arms or legs of a human or animal, or birds' wings
Muscles ➤ Joined to bones and help the bones move

Have a go! Touch your head and feel the hard skull inside. Bend your arm and clench your fists, making your muscles tighten.

Test yourself
1 What is another name for the backbone?
2 Name three animals with a hard shell.
3 What kind of skin does a snake have?

The human body

Do you know the names of the main parts of the body? Here they are.

Do you know any rhymes or songs about parts of the body? You could sing *Heads, shoulders, knees and toes*.

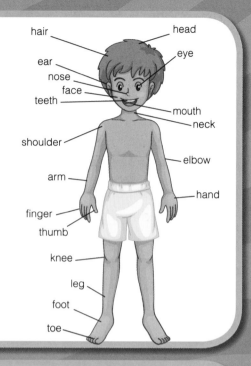

hair
head
eye
ear
nose
face
teeth
mouth
neck
shoulder
elbow
arm
hand
finger
thumb
knee
leg
foot
toe

The senses

Humans have **five senses**. They are **sight**, **smell**, **taste**, **touch** and **hearing**. Our senses help us to find out about the world around us. Which parts of the body do we use for each sense?

Eyes

Eyes are for seeing.

Eyes

Eyes can be different colours, such as blue, brown or green.

Eyelids and **eye lashes** help to keep eyes clean and moist.

Look carefully at the eyes of your friends and family; record the different colours.

Some people need **glasses** to help them see better.

Some people are **blind** – they cannot see at all. A lot of blind people have a guide dog.

Many people who cannot see read with their fingers. They feel special letters called **Braille**.

Close your eyes and find your way around. Think about what it must be like not to be able to see.

Keywords

Sight ➤ The ability to see

Braille ➤ The alphabet as a series of patterned dots raised on a page

Nose

The nose is for smelling. You breathe through your two nostrils. You can smell pleasant things like flowers, fruit and baking. What is your favourite smell? If you smell something nasty you might wrinkle your nose, or hold your nose. What is the worst smell you can think of?

Your sense of smell is useful. For example, a smell of smoke can be a warning of danger.

If you have a cold, you often lose your sense of smell as the nose gets blocked up.

Taste

The tongue is for tasting. You have tiny dots on your tongue. They are **taste buds**, which help you taste your food.

Top tip! Never poke anything into your ears because this could damage them. Never touch anything that may be hot like the cooker, a pan, a match, or a sparkler that has just finished burning.

Touch

The sense of touch is in the skin.

There are lots of opposite words to do with touch. For example:

- **hard** and **soft**
- **rough** and **smooth**
- **wet** and **dry**
- **hot** and **cold**

You feel a lot with your fingers, but other parts of your body can feel too.

For example:
- if you fall over, your knee might feel pain
- if someone touches your chin with a feather, it tickles.

Hearing

Ears are for hearing. If you go outside and listen carefully, you can hear many sounds: birds, traffic, a dog barking, children playing.

Loud noises like a dog barking might make you jump. Sounds that are close to you seem loud, but if you are far away they seem quieter.

A hearing aid can help if you are hard of hearing. People who cannot hear are **deaf**.

Have a go! Use the 'touch' words above to describe what these things feel like:

a tree trunk
an ice cube
a teddy bear
a flower petal
a tomato.

Test yourself

❶ How many senses are there? What are they called?

❷ What are the tiny dots on your tongue called?

❸ Why do you need eyelids?

❹ Which animal sometimes helps people who cannot see?

Animals, Including Humans

All animals have babies that grow into adults. This happens in many different ways.

Mammals

Mammal babies develop inside their mothers. Sometimes, the mother has more than one baby developing inside her. Two babies are **twins**. Mammal babies feed on milk.

Human babies:

- are completely helpless when they are born and they need looking after
- go through stages to become an adult:

baby ⟶ toddler ⟶ child ⟶ teenager ⟶ adult

- sometimes grow to look similar to their parents.

Other baby mammals have different names. For example:

- lamb (sheep)
- calf (cow, whale, dolphin)
- kitten (cat, rabbit)
- puppy (dog)
- cub (fox, bear)

Here are some interesting facts about baby mammals.

- Some baby mammals, such as puppies, kittens and mice, are born without hair. Their eyes do not open for one or two weeks.
- A guinea pig's eyes are open when it is born.
- Some baby mammals in the wild, such as elephants and zebras, have to walk as soon as they are born. This is because of predators.
- Whale and dolphin calves are born in the ocean.

Birds

Birds, including chickens, ducks and geese, lay eggs. Their chicks, ducklings or goslings hatch out of the egg.

A baby bird ready to fly the nest is called a **fledgling**.

This is how a chicken egg grows into an adult:

egg ⟶ chick ⟶ chicken

Then the cycle continues.

Top tip! Always have a magnifying glass handy to look closely at living things.

Amphibians

In spring, frogs lay **frogspawn** in pond water.

This is how frogs grow to an adult:

frogspawn ⟶ tadpole ⟶ frog

Then the cycle continues.

Reptiles

Crocodiles and turtles lay their eggs on land, often well away from water. The babies look like their parents but are tiny.

Fish

Fish lay eggs in rivers, lakes and seas. The eggs hatch into tiny fish and slowly grow into adult fish.

Insects

Butterflies lay eggs. The egg grows into a butterfly by going through these stages:

egg $\longrightarrow$ caterpillar $\longrightarrow$ **pupa** $\longrightarrow$ butterfly

Then the cycle continues.

Other insects, like moths, flies and ladybirds, change in a similar way.

Keywords

Frogspawn ➤ A tiny egg inside a blob of jelly

Pupa ➤ An insect at the stage between caterpillar and adult, when it has a hard covering

Vivarium ➤ A container to keep animals in

Working scientifically

The life cycle of a butterfly

1. Look for caterpillar or moth eggs in summer. They are usually laid on the underside of a leaf and are often in clusters. You can find them on cabbages, privet, hawthorn and other plants.

2. Bring home the eggs still on the leaf, with some more leaves on a twig.

3. Place the leaves and eggs into a large glass jar or **vivarium**.

4. Close the top, but leave air holes.

5. Watch the eggs hatch out into caterpillars.

6. Feed them with the same kind of leaves until they stop eating and make their own pupa.

7. Look at the pupas every day until the caterpillars or moths hatch out. When they can fly, let them go!

8. Record and date each change that you see.

Have a go!

Look at photos of yourself when you were a baby. Notice how much you have changed. Did you have teeth then? Has the colour of your eyes changed? Do you look like any other member of your family? In what way?

Test yourself

1. What is frogspawn?
2. What is a baby cow called?
3. Name a pet animal whose eyes are open when born.
4. Name two mammals whose babies are born in the ocean.

All animals, including humans, need three things to survive: **air**, **water** and **food**.

Air

All animals need air to breathe. Without air they would die.

Mammals that live on land breathe in and out through their mouth and nose. The air goes into the **lungs**. Humans need clean air to stay healthy. Traffic fumes, factory fumes and smoke can be harmful if you breathe them in.

Whales, dolphins and porpoises can go under water for quite a long time, but they must come up for air. They breathe through a **blowhole** on the top of their heads.

Fish breathe through their **gills**.

Young frogs (tadpoles) have gills, like fish. As they grow, they develop lungs. The adult frogs breathe through their nostrils with their mouths closed. They can also breathe through their skin.

Water

What do humans have in common with plants? Both plants and animals need water to survive!

Without water, your body would stop working properly. A human cannot survive for more than a few days without water.

Some animals can last a long time without water. They store it in their bodies or get water from leaves that they eat.

For example: camel   kangaroo rat   giraffe   koala

Water helps you:

- fight off illness because it washes away germs
- digest your food
- get rid of waste in your sweat and when you go to the toilet.

There is water in everything you drink. For example, fruit juices, milk, squash and fizzy drinks.

There is also water in many things that you **eat**. For example, fruit and vegetables such as oranges, peaches, tomatoes and celery.

Contaminated water can make you very ill. In countries where there is poor sanitation, many people die from drinking dirty water.

Food

All animals need food. As we have already learned, different animals eat different things. They are split into **carnivores**, **herbivores** and **omnivores**.

Humans can survive without food for a week or more, but people really need to eat every day to stay healthy. It is important to eat a variety of food. You should also try to eat healthily and not too much.

Top tip! Drink plenty of water. If you feel really thirsty, that usually means you should have been drinking more. It is a sign that your body needs water.

Shelter

Animals, including humans, need shelter to protect them from the weather or from danger.

Working scientifically

Breathing experiment

1. Sit quietly.
2. Count how many breaths you take in one minute. Write the number down.
3. Now run around for a few minutes. Are you out of breath? Are you breathing faster?
4. Sit down quietly again.
5. Count how many breaths you take in one minute. Write the number down.
6. You should count a higher number of breaths in one minute after you have been running around. Why do you think this is?

Keywords

Lungs ➤ Two spongy sacks inside the chest

Blowhole ➤ A hole in the top of the head of whales, dolphins and porpoises which acts as their nostril

Gills ➤ On the sides of a fish's head. The fish breathes through them

Contaminated ➤ Unclean, polluted or poisoned

Have a go! Name and draw three animals that breathe through a blowhole.

Test yourself

1. What are the three main things that all animals need to survive?
2. Which animals breathe through gills?
3. Name something that can be harmful to your lungs.

All humans need to eat to survive. It is important to know which foods are good for us and which ones we should eat less of.

Listen up

12

Protein, vitamins and energy foods

Here are some foods made from milk:

cream

yogurt

cheese

butter

Milk, yogurt and cheese help to keep our bones and teeth strong. Most of the milk we drink comes from cows. We can also drink milk from goats, sheep and other mammals. Human babies and other mammals can drink milk from their mothers.

Protein foods help keep our hair and skin healthy, and make our muscles grow.

- Some protein foods come from **animals**.
  For example: milk, meat, fish, seafood, eggs and cheese.
- Some protein foods come from **plants**.
  For example: nuts, peanut butter, soya milk, dried apricots and peas.

What other foods help us to be healthy?

Foods containing **vitamins** include:

- **fruit**: for example, apples, oranges, pears, peaches, bananas, plums, tomatoes
- **vegetables**: for example, cabbages, carrots, broccoli, leeks and lettuces.

We also need food to give us **energy**, so we can work and play without getting too tired. For example: potatoes, bread, rice, pasta and sugar.

Keywords

Protein ➤ Helps our bodies to grow and our muscles to become strong

Vitamins ➤ Help us to make the best use of our food and to fight diseases

Energy ➤ The power to do things; what keeps us active and alert

Sugar and fat

Sugar is high in energy. We should not eat too much of it. If we eat more sugar than we need, it might make us overweight or cause tooth decay.

Some foods have a lot of sugar in them. For example: sweets, chocolate, biscuits, cake and fizzy drinks.

Fats provide plenty of energy. We should not eat too many fatty foods.

Some foods have a lot of fat in them. For example: crisps, chips, burgers, fried food, pizza, cakes and biscuits.

You should try to have a mixed diet without eating too much of anything, especially fatty or sugary foods.

Exercise

Whatever we eat, we all need exercise. It helps to make our muscles and bones stronger. It also makes us breathe faster and allows more oxygen into our blood.

Some exercise is quite gentle, such as:

- walking to school
- playing outside
- walking in the countryside.

Some exercise is more energetic, such as:

- swimming
- football
- running
- gymnastics
- cycling.

Try to take some exercise every day.

Hygiene

Hygiene is about keeping clean and keeping disease away.

It is very important to:

- wash your hands often, especially before eating, after going to the toilet and after handling pets
- have baths or showers regularly to wash the rest of your body
- clean your teeth regularly, to brush away food that might make them decay.

 **Have a go!** Make a chart of what you eat each day for a week. Circle everything that you think is a healthy food.

 **Test yourself**

1. Name two things that might happen if you eat too much sugar.
2. Which other kind of food might not be good for you if you eat too much of it?
3. What three things should you do for good hygiene?

This mind map will help you remember all the main points from this topic. Have a go at drawing your own mind map.

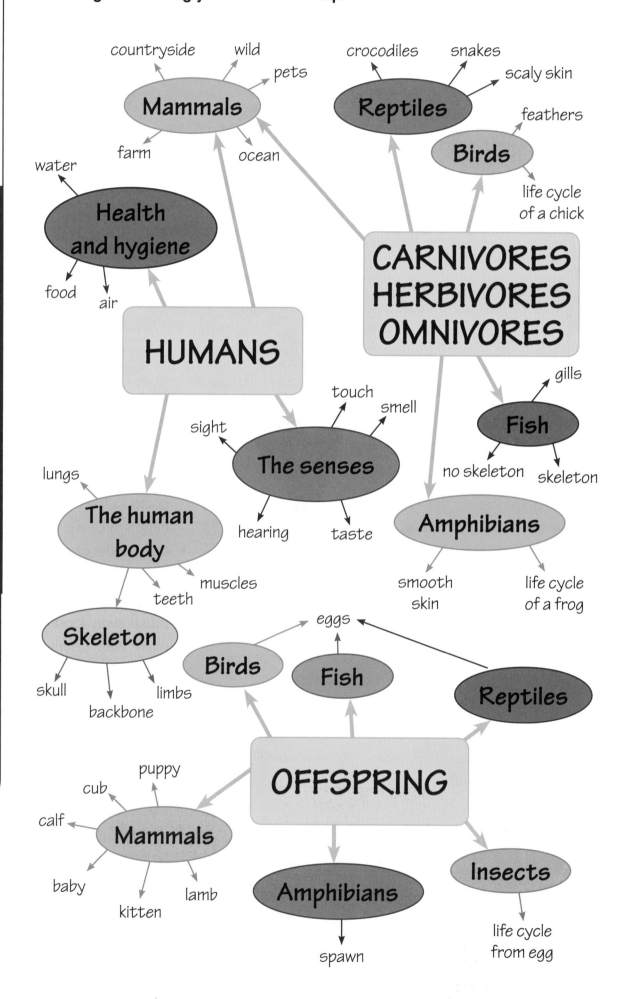

1 **a.** What is a carnivore?   **(1 mark)**

....

b. What is a herbivore?   **(1 mark)**

....

2 **a.** Name three kinds of limbs.   **(3 marks)**

....

b. Underline the three animals that have no limbs.   **(3 marks)**

horse   snake   bee   spider   shark   elephant   dolphin   mouse

3 Name two animals that have eight limbs.   **(2 marks)**

....

4 Draw a line to link each of the five senses with the correct part of the body.   **(5 marks)**

eyes		taste
ears		smell
nose		sight
mouth/tongue		touch
skin		hearing

5 What is a pupa?   **(1 mark)**

....

....

6 What three things do animals need in order to stay alive?   **(3 marks)**

....

7 Circle three foods that contain a lot of sugar.   **(3 marks)**

fish   nuts   cakes   milk   fizzy drinks   carrots   chocolate

8 Underline three foods that contain a lot of fat.   **(3 marks)**

apples   chips   pizza   egg   dried apricots   crisps   cabbage

listen up 13

All around us there are lots of:

- living things
- things that were once alive but are now dead
- things that have never been alive.

Living things

Here is a chart to show what animals and plants need and do to stay alive.

Animals	Animals and plants	Plants
• develop from an egg or baby • should eat a balanced diet • need air to breathe • have babies or lay eggs • walk, run, slither, crawl, swim, climb • touch and feel • get rid of waste (go to the toilet)	• grow and change • need water • need food • need air, warmth and light • reproduce • move	• grow from a seed or bulb • make their own food • need warmth and light to grow • grow more plants • flower heads turn to face the sun

So all living things **eat and drink**, **move about**, **breathe**, **touch and feel**, **grow and change**, **get rid of waste** and **have babies**.

Here are some living things you might see:

tree   flower   child   cat   worm   butterfly

Things that were alive but are now dead

Remember, things that were once living but are now dead must have been alive once, so they must be a plant or animal. For example:

| wilted flower | old log | dead woodlouse | dry grass | shell | bone |

Things that have never been alive

There are lots of things that have never been alive. For example:

| rock | house | bottle | car | lorry | can | moon |

How can you tell if things have never been alive? Ask yourself these questions.

- Can a rock breathe? Does it need air?
- Do plastic bottles make young plastic bottles?
- Do cars and lorries grow and change?
- Do stars drink water?

The answer to these questions is no.
So they have never been alive!

Top tip! If you find it hard to put an object into the correct group, think of some more questions. For example, does a house need to eat? Does a brick move?

Have a go! Wherever you are this weekend, write down or draw all the things you can see that are a. living, b. were living but are now dead, c. have never been alive.

Sort them into groups. Which group has the most things in it?

Test yourself

❶ Name the seven things that animals do to show that they are living.

❷ How do you know that a bucket is not alive?

❸ Circle the five things that are alive.

dog   money   fence
human   tree   shoe
chimney   baby   rose

Living things need a **habitat** where they can live, grow and **breed**.

Different habitats suit different animals and plants.

Animals

Animals need a habitat where they can live, grow and breed. Most need **shelter** from the weather or from danger. They need a place where their young can be born.

Animals find their natural habitat in many different places. They choose a habitat that is best for them.

You may find animals' habitats:

- underground
- in water
- in a nest
- up a tree
- under bushes and leaves
- under a log.

Pets, zoo animals and farm animals live where they are looked after by humans. They might live:

- in a cage
- in a tank
- in a house
- in a garden
- in a field
- in a barn.

Other habitats include:

- the ocean, where fish and mammals live in deep, cool, dark water
- the rainforest, where animals and exotic birds live in the hot, wet jungle
- the seashore, where shellfish, crabs and seabirds live at the edge of salt water.

Parent tip! Help your child use the Internet and books to find out about plant and animal habitats.

Keywords

Habitat ➤ The natural home or environment of an animal, plant or other living thing
Breed ➤ To grow more plants or animals, e.g. from seeds or eggs

Plants

Many cultivated plants live in gardens. This is their habitat.

Some plants grow in any soil. Others grow only in one kind of soil. Different places have different types of soil. For example:

- sandy
- clay
- stony
- chalky.

Some plants need strong sunlight. Others grow best in shady places. Wild flowers grow where the habitat is best for them. For example:

- woods
- gardens
- in water
- in sand
- fields
- by a pond
- by the roadside.

Plants and animals

Plants and animals depend on each other.

Herbivores and omnivores, including birds, eat plants and seeds.

Some plants need animals to distribute their seeds for them.

- Sometimes a bird or animal carries seeds in its feathers or fur, then the seeds drop onto the ground.
- Sometimes a bird or animal eats a seed or berry. This passes through them and falls to the ground in their droppings. The next spring the seed grows into a new plant.

Have a go!

Look at a patch of ground near where you live. Use books or the Internet to help you check what plants grow well there.

Do the same with another patch of ground. What similarities and differences are there?

Test yourself

1. Which two main things do animals shelter from in their habitat?
2. What is the meaning of the word breed?
3. Circle four places which are habitats for animals:

    underground   inside a car
    a rainforest   up a tree   in the ocean

4. Name three creatures that live on the seashore.

Human habitats

Most humans live in a house, bungalow, flat, caravan or tent. A few live in a castle or on a boat!

Our habitat gives us:

- **shelter** from the weather – imagine having to sleep out of doors in wet weather or in winter
- **warmth** – central heating or a fire in cold weather
- **comfort** – a bedroom, bed, chairs
- **our favourite things** – books, toys, games, television, electronic equipment
- **food** and **water**.

Plant habitats

Where do plants grow best?

Trees sometimes grow in big groups like a forest. Some grow on their own.

Parent tip! If possible, let your child use a microscope. This will give them an even closer look at animals and plants.

Plants grow in the habitat that best suits them. For example:

- bluebells grow in shady woods
- poppies grow in sunny fields
- roses grow in gardens with a mix of shade and sun
- bulrushes grow by a pond
- water lilies grow in a pond
- dandelions grow almost anywhere
- cacti grow in dry, sandy places
- seaweed grows in or near the sea.

Animal habitats

Adult animals spend most of their time looking for food, feeding, breeding and caring for their young.

There are many animal habitats. Here are a few of them.

- **Up trees** – squirrels make a **drey** in the branches of a tree.
- **Under bushes and leaves** – hedgehogs hibernate for the winter.
- **In old buildings** – mice shelter and make nests.
- **Nests** – in spring, birds build their nests and lay eggs in lots of different places:
    - in gardens, fields and woods
    - in bushes and trees
    - on cliffs
    - in old buildings.

Animal habitats (continued)

- **Underground** – rabbits make tunnels and rooms to live underground. This is called a **warren**.
  Badgers also make tunnels and rooms that spread a long way underground. This is called a **sett**. Foxes make a **den** or '**earth**' under tree roots, under a shed or even in a pile of rubbish!

Entrance to a badger sett

Micro-habitats

Woodlice under a log

Here is information about **micro-habitats**.

- **Under a log** – small animals such as insects may be found under logs. Some are so tiny they can hardly be seen, except with a magnifying glass or a microscope.
  For example: woodlice, spiders, mites, beetles, slugs, snails, millipedes, centipedes and worms. Snakes and amphibians sometimes rest or sleep under a large log.
- **In a pond** – fish, amphibians and many species of pond life live in a micro-habitat in water. Fish and amphibians can be seen and studied with the naked eye, but microscopic creatures are there too.

Other micro-habitats are **in a compost heap**, **under tree bark**, **a stone** or **in a rock pool**.

Keyword

Micro-habitat ➤ A miniature habitat within a larger one; an area where the environment is different from the world around it

Listen up 15

Have a go!

Find a dead log and gently roll it over.
Draw or write about any animals or plants you see.
Roll the log back.
At home, find out about each animal or plant.

Test yourself

1. Explain why your home is a good habitat for you.
2. What is another name for a fox's den?
3. Which animal builds a drey in a tree?
4. Name a plant that grows in shady places.

Listen up 16

All animals, including humans, need to eat, whether they are herbivore, carnivore or omnivore.

Where does our food come from?

We buy food in supermarkets, smaller shops and markets, but that is not where the food comes from.

- Fruit and vegetables grow on trees and smaller plants, or underground.
- Seeds and nuts, herbs and spices, sugar and flour, potatoes and rice come from plants.
- Meat comes from animals. For example, sheep, cow, deer, chicken.
- Milk, cheese and butter come from mammals such as cows, sheep and goats.
- Eggs come from hens, ducks, geese or other birds.

Where does the food for animals come from? They get their food from plants and other smaller animals. Smaller animals eat plants or even smaller creatures!

The food chain

The food that humans and animals eat is in a food chain. This means that a plant or animal is eaten by a different animal, which is eaten by another one, and so on.

There are a lot of different food chains. Some are longer than others.

For example:

grass is eaten by a cow $\longrightarrow$ the cow's meat is eaten by humans

A food chain is sometimes shown like this:

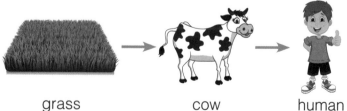

grass   cow   human

Examples of food chains

Here are some examples of food chains:

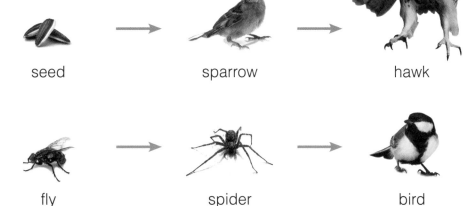

seed → sparrow → hawk

fly → spider → bird

Bigger, stronger animals like humans, lions and raptors are often at the top of the food chain.

Top tip! Think carefully about what you eat, where each food comes from and its food chain. Food that comes from a plant does not have its own food chain.

Have a go! Choose a carnivore. Draw and name it. Make a food chain for it.

How many stages are there in the food chain?

Try this with as many different carnivores as you can.

Test yourself

1 Put these in the right order for a food chain.

fox   dandelion   rabbit

2 Underline the five animals that are at the top of the food chain.

mouse   human   eagle
worm   tiger   rabbit
lion   killer whale

3 Circle the five food items that come from plants.

eggs   potatoes   rice
milk   nuts   sugar
cheese   flour

This mind map will help you remember all the main points from this topic. Have a go at drawing your own mind map.

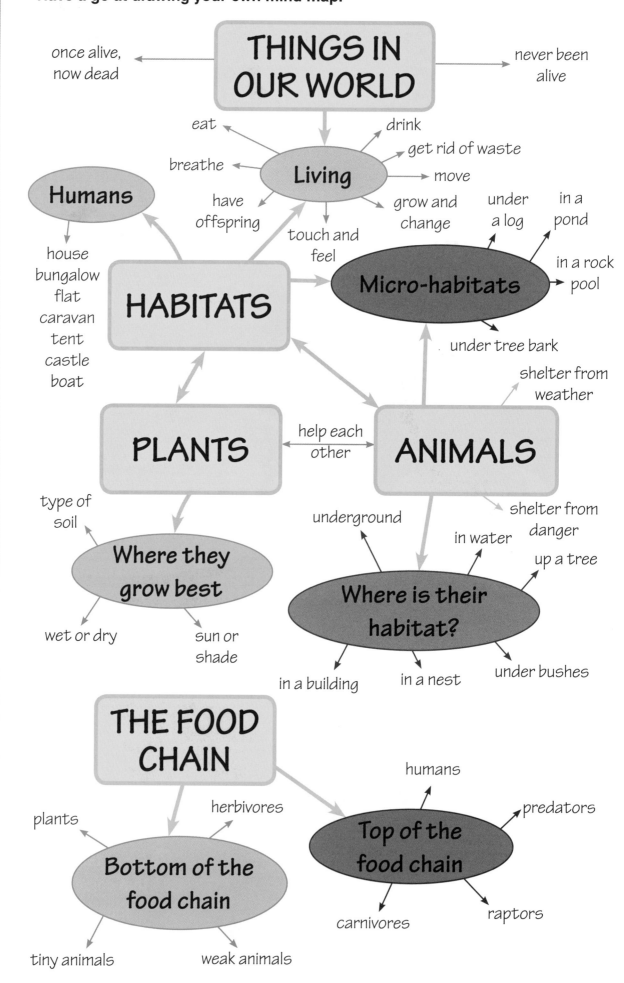

THINGS IN OUR WORLD

once alive, now dead

never been alive

Living — eat, drink, get rid of waste, move, grow and change, touch and feel, have offspring, breathe

Humans — house, bungalow, flat, caravan, tent, castle, boat

HABITATS

Micro-habitats — under a log, in a pond, in a rock pool, under tree bark, shelter from weather

PLANTS — help each other — ANIMALS — shelter from danger

Where they grow best — type of soil, wet or dry, sun or shade

Where is their habitat? — underground, in water, up a tree, under bushes, in a nest, in a building

THE FOOD CHAIN

Bottom of the food chain — plants, herbivores, tiny animals, weak animals

Top of the food chain — humans, predators, raptors, carnivores

1 Underline four things that are alive. **(4 marks)**

bone   flower   car   cat   holly tree   shell   table   hedgehog   pencil

2 Tick (✓) the boxes next to the correct statements. **(2 marks)**

Rocks have never been alive.

Rocks are alive.

A shell is alive.

A shell was once alive, now dead.

3 What is a habitat? **(1 mark)**

....

....

4 Name a plant that grows in a pond. .... **(1 mark)**

5 Name a plant that grows in the desert. .... **(1 mark)**

6 Circle two animals that make their home underground. **(2 marks)**

squirrel   rabbit   hedgehog   horse   badger   frog

7 What do you use a microscope for? **(1 mark)**

....

8 Name four foods we make from the foodstuff we get from cows. **(4 marks)**

....

....

9 Put this food chain into the right order: **(1 mark)**

frog ⟶ heron ⟶ fly

.... ⟶ .... ⟶ ....

10 Name two living things at the bottom of the food chain. **(2 marks)**

....

All **objects** have names and are made of many different **materials**.

Objects at home

At home, you might have objects such as a table, a kettle, windows, cups, lunchboxes and books.

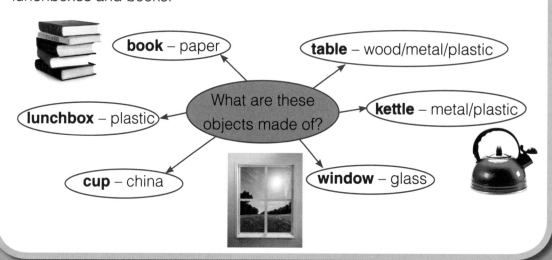

book – paper

table – wood/metal/plastic

lunchbox – plastic

What are these objects made of?

kettle – metal/plastic

cup – china

window – glass

Clothes

Your clothes are objects too, and they have names.

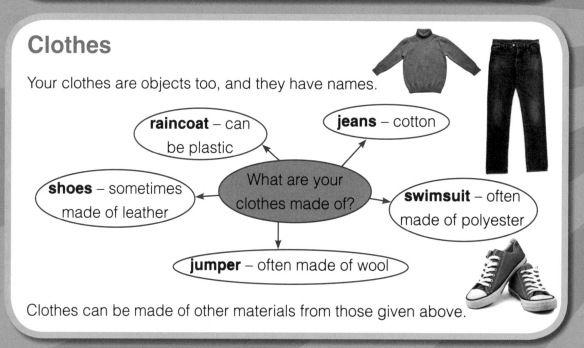

raincoat – can be plastic

jeans – cotton

shoes – sometimes made of leather

What are your clothes made of?

swimsuit – often made of polyester

jumper – often made of wool

Clothes can be made of other materials from those given above.

Parent tip! Encourage your child to work out the materials that objects are made of. Give hints about what different materials are like (e.g. bendy, soft, hard).

Keywords

Object ➤ A thing

Material ➤ What objects are made of

Objects outside home

Outside your house, the objects have a name. For example, fence, wall, pavement, dustbin and car.

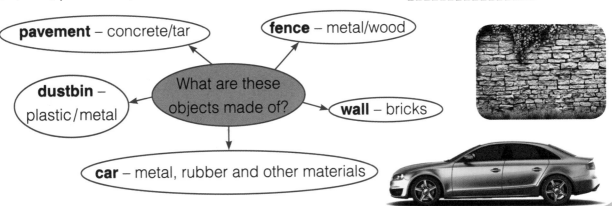

pavement – concrete/tar

fence – metal/wood

dustbin – plastic/metal

What are these objects made of?

wall – bricks

car – metal, rubber and other materials

Objects at school

At school, there are also objects. For example, coat peg, wash basin, pencil and exercise book.

exercise book – paper and metal (can you see the tiny metal parts, the staples that hold the book together?)

What are these objects made of?

coat peg – metal

wash basin – metal/porcelain

pencil – wood and graphite (the graphite part is what we often call the 'lead' through the middle of the pencil)

Have a go!

Choose ten objects from home. Name them – ask an adult if you are not sure.

See if you can guess what each object is made of.

Draw and label the objects, and write down the materials they are made of.

Test yourself

1 What is another word for an object?

2 What does the word material mean?

3 What is a kettle made of?

4 Underline five objects that can be made of wood.

chair   toilet   fence
chimney   table   door
coat   cupboard

You now know a range of materials.

For example:

wood   metal   plastic   porcelain   bricks
glass   graphite   china   polyester   cotton
wool   leather   concrete   tar   rubber

The picture shows **rubber tapping**.

Some materials are **natural**.
Others are made (**manufactured**).

Natural materials

Sometimes it is hard to tell whether an object is made of natural materials.

Here are some natural materials.

leather   wool   cotton   oil

wood   stone   sand

These materials all come from different places.

- **Leather** is the skin of animals.
- **Wool** is the thick coat of animals such as sheep, alpacas and goats.
- **Cotton** grows on plants.
- **Oil** comes from sea creatures that lived millions of years ago.
- **Wood** comes from trees.
- **Stone** and **sand** are dug out of the ground in places called **quarries**.
- The **sand** on the beach is made of bits of rock and shellfish.

Other natural materials dug out of the ground are:

- clay
- diamonds and other precious stones such as emeralds, rubies and sapphires
- metals such as iron, gold, silver, tin and copper.

So a diamond ring is natural!

Manufactured materials

Many objects are manufactured. This means that people change natural materials and make them into something different.

Did you know?
- Glass is made of sand.
- Most plastic materials are made of oil.
- Plates, cups and pottery vases are made of clay.
- Bricks are made from clay.
- Paper is made of wood. Some paper is made of old clothes and **recycled** paper.

18

Top tip! When you look at objects, try to work out which group they belong to: natural or manufactured.

Keywords

Natural ➤ Materials that come from nature; they are not made by humans

Manufactured ➤ Made by people who change a natural material to make it into something completely different, usually in combination with other things

Quarry ➤ A deep hole where stones and sand are dug out of the ground

Recycled ➤ When the material an object is made from is used again

Have a go! Put ten things from around the house into two groups: natural or manufactured. Record what you have collected. Which do you have more of?

Was it easier to find objects made of natural or manufactured materials? Why do you think that is?

Test yourself

❶ Circle the four materials that are dug out of the ground.

wood   stone   clay
plastic   wool   silver
leather   rubies

❷ Underline the natural materials.

plastic   wool   oil
glass   sand   wood
paper   diamond

❸ Where does cotton come from?

All materials, whether they are natural or manufactured, have **properties**. The properties of a material tell us what the material is like.

Words that describe materials

To describe the properties of materials, you can use opposites.

Is the material:

- hard or soft?

- rough or smooth?

- heavy or light?

- shiny or dull?

- **absorbent** or not absorbent?

Here are some other opposites:
- solid/liquid
- stretchy/stiff
- hot/cold
- **opaque/transparent**
- firm/bendy
- waterproof/not waterproof.

Properties of some materials

Here are the properties of some common materials.

- **Wood** is usually **hard** and **strong**.
- **Metal** feels **cold** and is even **harder** and **stronger** than wood.
- **Plastic** is **waterproof**, is sometimes **bendy** and can be **opaque** or **transparent**.

Top tip! You can have great fun feeling the texture of materials, but never touch knives or other sharp objects, or anything that is hot. Never touch plugs or sockets. They can be very dangerous.

Keywords

Properties ➤ What a material is like; for example, hard, soft

Absorbent ➤ It will soak up liquid

Opaque ➤ Not see-through

Transparent ➤ See-through

Texture ➤ What the surface of an object feels like

Using your senses

You use two senses to find out about the properties of materials: **touch** and **sight**.

- **Feel** the **texture** of a material. Is it warm or cold? Describe what you feel, using as many different words as you can.

- **Look** carefully at a material. Think about what it is made of. Which of the words in the box on the previous page describe the material?

Have a go! Think of some everyday materials and talk about their properties. Use opposites and think of other words to describe them, too.

Test yourself

1. Which two senses do you use to find out the texture of different materials?
2. Tick (✓) the box next to the correct sentence.

   Wood is light and bendy. ☐

   Wood is strong and hard. ☐

3. Name the opposite of:

   a. shiny

   b. heavy

   c. rough.

Putting materials in sets

We can group materials by their properties. Some materials will be in more than one **set**. Here are some sets of objects made of different materials.

Hard

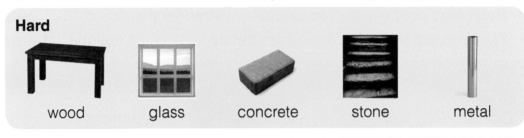

| wood | glass | concrete | stone | metal |

Shiny

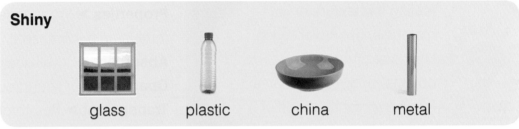

| glass | plastic | china | metal |

Transparent

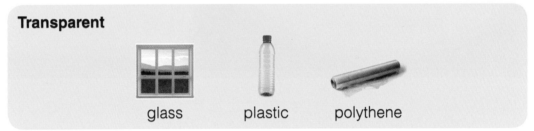

| glass | plastic | polythene |

Glass is in all three sets because it is **hard**, **shiny** and **transparent**.

Here are some more groups of materials according to their properties.

Soft
- feather
- wool
- cotton wool

Light
- feather
- paper
- cotton wool

Bendy
- rubber
- flower stem
- feather

Strong
- metal
- wood
- rock

A **feather** is **soft** and **light** and **bendy**.
Metal can be **hard**, **shiny** and **strong**.
Cotton wool is **soft** and **light**.

Listen up 20

Keyword

Set ➤ Another word for group

Toys

Toy makers choose materials with the most suitable properties for making certain toys. Look at your toys and feel them. You will see that they are made from many different materials with many different properties.

Examples of properties: soft   hard   bendy   heavy

There are many other words you can use to describe toys' properties. Can you think of some?

Working scientifically

Materials for making an umbrella

What you need

- paper
- polythene
- cotton material
- aluminium foil
- plastic
- wool

What to do

Do this experiment in the garden or the bath!

1 Pretend you want to make a new umbrella.

2 Think about whether the umbrella should be heavy or light, thick or thin.

3 Talk about which of the materials above might be suitable for your umbrella. You need the material for your umbrella to be **waterproof** and **not absorbent**.

4 Find out if you are right by pouring water over each material in turn.

Try doing experiments to find the best material for other objects, such as a cushion, or a pair of slippers, or a toy box.

Top tip! Danger! Never put polythene over your face as you will not be able to breathe. Make sure an adult knows you are using it.

Have a go! Look for five objects outside. Draw them. Write the material(s) they are made of and two properties for each one.

Test yourself

1 Which three properties does glass have?

2 Name three things that are the opposite of heavy.

3 Use three words to describe the properties of a rock.

4 Name three materials that are shiny.

Some materials are wrong for certain things. Imagine a saucepan made of paper or a bucket made of wool!

Manufacturers choose the right materials for making things because they know the properties of the materials.

One object can be made of different materials

Sometimes an object can be made from lots of different materials.

For example:

- a **spoon** can be made of **plastic**, **metal**, **wood** or **pottery**
- a **chair** can be made of **metal**, **wood**, **plastic** or a **mixture of materials**
- a **wall** can be made of **brick**, **stone**, **concrete** or **glass**.

Materials suitable for more than one object

Some materials have many uses. For example: metal, glass, plastic, wood, cotton, leather, bricks and paper.

Let's look at metal and glass.

Metal has many uses. For example: door handles, coins, cars, cans, gates and screws.

Look at the metal things around you. Why is metal a suitable material for these things?

- It is strong.
- It lasts a long time.
- It is waterproof.
- It can be made into different shapes.

Can you think of any other reasons?

Glass has many uses too.

For example: windows, mirrors, bottles, shower doors, lenses and tumblers.

Look at the glass things around you. Why is glass a suitable material for these things?

- It is transparent.
- It can be cleaned easily.
- It is strong, as long as it is used properly.

Fascinating facts

- Nobody knows who first made glass from sand thousands of years ago.
- In the nineteenth century, John Boyd Dunlop invented an inflatable tyre for his son's bicycle. The tyre covered the hard metal wheels and, thanks to Dunlop, made cycling a lot more comfortable!
- Another nineteenth-century inventor, Alexander Parkes, invented one of the earliest forms of plastic.
- Also in the nineteenth century, Charles Macintosh experimented with materials and came up with the best waterproof material for a raincoat – now called a mackintosh or just mac!

Many materials were developed or invented in the nineteenth century. That is less than two hundred years ago. Imagine what life must have been like without plastic, without inflatable tyres on your bike, and with no waterproof coat to wear!

Parent tip! Use the Internet or books to find out about these inventors, and about others who developed materials that are used today.

Keywords

Manufacturers ➤ People who make things for us to buy; this is often done in a factory

Top tip! Danger! Remember, broken glass can cut you.

Have a go! Make a list of objects made from wood and plastic.

Why do you think each material is suitable for the examples you have listed?

It might help to think about why a material might not be suitable; for example, why you would not use a cardboard box for keeping a goldfish.

Test yourself

1. Circle four things that a wall can be made of.

   brick   feathers   stone
   concrete   cotton
   glass   shells

2. How do manufacturers choose the right materials for making things?

3. Name three things a spoon can be made of.

4. Underline five things that can be made of metal.

   coin   window   raincoat
   saucepan   gate   toothbrush
   screw   door handle

Materials can be used as they are or changed. You can change the shape of lots of things with your hands.

For example, you can:

- flatten
- fold
- bend
- twist
- squash
- stretch.

Let's look at some other ways that materials can change.

Heating and cooling

Glass

Glass is made of sand. It can be many shapes and different sizes.

Glass is heated to very high temperatures to make it **soft**.

Then it can be:

- flattened and cut to make windows
- blown to make bottles, jars and vases
- poured into a mould to make different shapes.

When the glass **cools** down, it becomes **hard** again.

Plastic

Plastic also goes soft or melts when it is heated. This is how it is made into all kinds of bottles, toys, boxes and many other objects. It sets hard when it is cooled.

Water

Water is a liquid. When it is heated it turns into steam (a gas). When frozen, it becomes **ice** (a solid).

Chocolate

Chocolate is a **solid**. When heated, it melts into a **liquid**.

Keywords

Liquid ➤ Flows freely

Steam ➤ A gas, a white mist of water droplets in the air, which is formed when water is boiled

Solid ➤ A material that is firm and hard

Listen up 22

One-way change

Wood, **paper**, **clay** and **cement** all go through a one-way change.

Wood

Wood is changed in a range of ways. For example:

- it is sawn into planks for the floor or cut into shape for doors or table tops
- it can be carved with a sharp knife into any shape you like
- it can be chopped into logs and burned to keep you warm.

If you burn wood, it turns to **ash**. Unlike glass, chocolate, plastic and water, it cannot be changed back to how it was. So wood goes through a one-way change.

Paper

When paper is burned it goes through a one-way change into ash, like wood.

Clay

Clay can be moulded when it is moist and quite soft. When it dries, it gradually becomes hard. To make the clay even harder, it is fired in a kiln (a type of oven).

Lumps of clay are pushed into a mould to make bricks. They are also fired when they have dried out.

Cement

Cement begins as a powder. When sand and water is added, it becomes liquid and soft, and makes concrete. The concrete is used to make pavements and to fix bricks together. It sets very hard as it dries.

Keyword

Ash ➤ A grey or white powder that forms after materials like wood and paper are burned

Have a go!

You can fold, twist and screw paper up into a ball. Think of other ways you can change the shape of paper.

Have you ever tried origami? Ask an adult to help you make a paper hat or a paper aeroplane.

Test yourself

1 How does wood change when you burn it?

2 Name three materials that go soft when warmed.

3 What is origami?

4 What is added to cement powder to make it turn liquid, then set hard?

se experiments with liquids and solids.

Heating and cooling

You can do some easy experiments to find out about the properties of water.

Working scientifically

Steam and mirrors

1. With an adult, put cold water into a kettle and turn it on.

2. When the water boils, do you see steam coming from the spout?

3. Keep your hand well away from the steam. Hold a mirror above the kettle. See water droplets form on the mirror.

Freezing!

1. Pour cold water into a plastic container and put it into the freezer. Leave some room because the solid will expand.

2. After several hours, see if it has changed from a liquid to a solid. This solid is ice.

3. See what happens when you leave the ice in the room. How long does it take to melt and return to a liquid?

Butter is an opaque solid.

How butter changes

1. With an adult, put some butter into a pan and heat it.
2. Watch it change from solid to liquid and from opaque to transparent.
3. Will it change back to a solid when you cool it? Does it look the same as before?

Eggs come in a hard shell. When you break an egg, you see:

- a thick, transparent liquid called the egg white
- a round, opaque yolk, which is liquid but not as runny as the egg white.

1. Try frying your egg in a little fat. Watch the egg white change from liquid to solid and transparent to opaque in a few seconds. Does the yolk change as much?

2. Does the egg white stay opaque? If you fry the egg for a few minutes you will find that the yolk becomes solid, too. Do you think the egg white and yolk will change back to how they were?

Everyday Materials

Dissolving

Dissolving is when you mix something with a liquid until it becomes part of the liquid.

Here are two simple experiments you can do.

Working scientifically

Salt

1 Put a teaspoonful of salt into a glass of cold water and stir.

2 Watch what happens. Is the water cloudy? Is it clear? Does the salt **dissolve**?

Sugar

1 Put a teaspoonful of sugar into a glass of cold water and stir.

2 Does it dissolve in the same way as the salt?

3 What happens if you heat the water with the sugar in? Does the sugar dissolve then?

Listen up 23

Keyword

Dissolve ➤ Dissolving is when you mix something with a liquid until it seems to become part of the liquid

Top tip! Experiments are great fun. Always have an adult with you. Danger! Steam does not look as hot as fire, but it can burn.

Have a go! With an adult, put some chocolate into a saucepan and heat it gently. See how quickly it becomes liquid.

Melted chocolate is delicious when you pour it over ice cream. Watch the chocolate set hard and solid as it touches the freezing ice cream. Don't worry, it will go soft again in the warmth of your mouth!

Test yourself

1 How does egg white change when you heat it?

2 What happens when you freeze water?

3 Does butter go back to how it was after melting?

This mind map will help you remember all the main points from this topic. Have a go at drawing your own mind map.

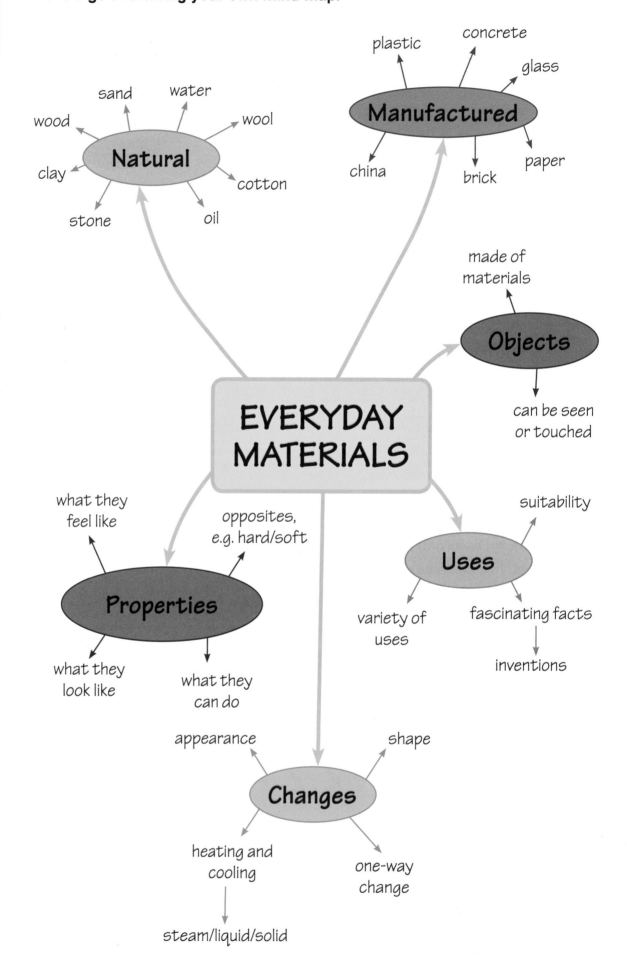

1 Draw a line between each object and the material it is made of. **(5 marks)**

frying pan		glass
cup		wood
mirror		plastic
lunchbox		clay
floorboard		metal

2 **a.** Where do diamonds come from? .... **(1 mark)**

b. Where does leather come from? .... **(1 mark)**

3 **a.** Name three things that paper can be made of. **(3 marks)**

....

....

....

b. What are bricks made of? .... **(1 mark)**

4 Name three words that describe the properties of glass. **(3 marks)**

....

....

....

5 Complete these sentences.

a. A book is made of .... **(1 mark)**

b. Windows are made of .... **(1 mark)**

6 **a.** How does chocolate change if you heat it? **(1 mark)**

....

b. How does paper change if you burn it? **(1 mark)**

....

Identifying and naming

1 Why should you leave wild flowers to grow and not pick them? **(1 mark)**

....

2 Are these flowers **wild** or **cultivated**? Write **w** or **c** next to each flower. **(4 marks)**

a. dandelion ....

c. sweet pea ....

b. pansy ....

d. clover ....

3 What does it mean if fruit and vegetables are **ripe**? **(1 mark)**

....

4 Circle the three 'vegetables' that are actually fruits. **(3 marks)**

banana   courgette   orange   pepper   cucumber   blackcurrant

5 Circle three fruits. **(3 marks)**

raspberry   potato   pear   lettuce   carrot   strawberry   parsnip

6 Fill in the gaps with the correct words. **(6 marks)**

needles   year   dark   autumn   shiny   leaves

Different kinds of trees have different-shaped ....

Deciduous trees lose their leaves in .... Evergreen

trees have leaves all .... round. Some evergreen

trees have .... and some have ....

green .... leaves.

Total — 18

Structure

1 In which season do wild flowers scatter their seeds?   **(1 mark)**

....

2 In which season will seeds begin to grow into plants?   **(1 mark)**

....

3 Fill in the gaps with the correct word.   **(3 marks)**

root	leaf	flower

a. Lettuce, cabbage and spinach are the .... of the plant.

b. Cauliflower and broccoli are the .... of a plant.

c. Carrots and parsnips are the .... of a plant.

4 Label the tree using the words below.

trunk   branch   twig   leaf   roots   **(5 marks)**

Total $\frac{}{10}$

How they grow

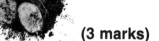

1 Name three vegetables that are bulbs. **(3 marks)**

....

2 Fill in the gaps with either **deciduous** or **evergreen**.

a. A horse chestnut tree is .... **(1 mark)**

b. A cedar tree is .... **(1 mark)**

c. A pine tree is .... **(1 mark)**

d. A beech tree is .... **(1 mark)**

3 What happens to a plant if it has no water? **(1 mark)**

....

4 Where are bulbs kept over winter? **(2 marks)**

....

5 Name the seed of a horse chestnut tree. **(1 mark)**

....

6 Name the seed of a pine tree. **(1 mark)**

....

7 Draw a circle. Draw and label the life cycle of a plant around
the circle, beginning and ending with the seed. **(5 marks)**
Use these stages in the correct order:

seed   stem and leaves   flower   roots and shoots   bud   seed

Total $\frac{}{17}$

The four seasons

1 In which season do most flowers grow? .... **(1 mark)**

2 In which season is the Sun at its highest in the sky? **(1 mark)**

....

3 In which season do animals and birds eat as much as they can before the cold weather comes? **(1 mark)**

....

4 In which season do trees give most shade from the Sun? **(1 mark)**

....

5 What does hibernation mean? **(1 mark)**

....

6 What does migration mean? **(1 mark)**

....

7 In which season do birds lay eggs? .... **(1 mark)**

8 In which season do leaves sprout from buds? **(1 mark)**

....

9 Draw a tree during each season. **(4 marks)**

spring	summer	autumn	winter

Total ___ / 12

The weather

❶ Fill in each gap with the correct word.

hail   sleet   snow   rain

a. Water droplets fall as .... in warm weather. **(1 mark)**

b. .... is pieces of frozen rain. **(1 mark)**

c. When rain contains some ice or snowflakes,

   it is called .... **(1 mark)**

d. The word .... describes tiny ice crystals
   that fall as white flakes. **(1 mark)**

❷ Tick (✔) the box next to the correct statement. **(3 marks)**

a. A reservoir is a large lake where water is stored.

   A reservoir is part of the sea where we can swim.

b. A hurricane is a gentle breeze.

   A hurricane is a strong wind that causes damage.

c. A rainbow appears when the Sun shines and it rains.

   A rainbow always appears in a heavy rain storm.

❸ Fill in the gaps with the correct words to complete these
sentences all about rain. **(7 marks)**

hands   watering   grow   drink   humans   drought   floods

Plants need rain to help them ....

Animals and birds need rain to ....

.... need water for drinking, washing .... ,

bathing, washing clothes and .... the garden.

If there is too much rain, there might be .... If there is

no rain for a long time, there will be a ....

Total ——
14

Identifying and naming

① Draw and label five mammals you could keep as a pet.　**(5 marks)**

② Name three amphibians you might find in a pond.　**(3 marks)**

....　.................................　.................................

③ Complete each sentence by writing the correct animal group.

mammal　bird　reptile　amphibian　fish　insect

a. A mole is a ....　**(1 mark)**

b. A dolphin is a ....　**(1 mark)**

c. A toad is an ....　**(1 mark)**

d. An eagle is a ....　**(1 mark)**

e. A snake is a ....　**(1 mark)**

f. A bear is a ....　**(1 mark)**

g. A butterfly is an ....　**(1 mark)**

h. A shark is a ....　**(1 mark)**

i. An ostrich is a ....　**(1 mark)**

j. A turtle is a ....　**(1 mark)**

Total $\frac{}{18}$

Animals, Including Humans

What they eat

1 What does a baleen whale eat? **(1 mark)**

....

2 Name two things that a killer whale might eat. **(2 marks)**

....

3 What is another name for a killer whale? **(1 mark)**

....

4 How is the killer whale different from the baleen whale? **(1 mark)**

....

5 What do owls eat? **(1 mark)**

....

6 What makes a wolf an omnivore? **(1 mark)**

....

7 Some humans are herbivores. What are they called? **(1 mark)**

....

8 Fill in the gaps with the correct words.

 a herbivore **a carnivore** **an omnivore**

a. A tiger is .... **(1 mark)**

b. A panda is .... **(1 mark)**

c. A tadpole is .... **(1 mark)**

d. A frog is .... **(1 mark)**

e. A crocodile is .... **(1 mark)**

f. A bear is .... **(1 mark)**

g. A rabbit is .... **(1 mark)**

Total $\frac{}{15}$

Structure

1 Label the parts of the skeleton. **(12 marks)**

vertebrae   arm   leg   skull   foot   hand   fingers
toes   ribs   knee   elbow   pelvis

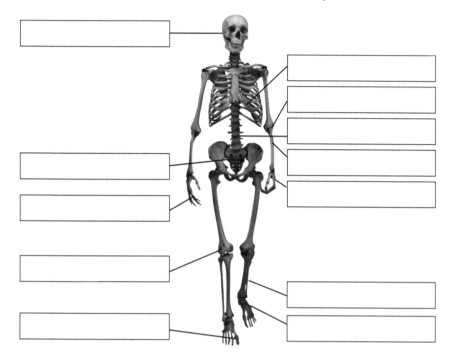

2 Name three kinds of limbs. **(3 marks)**

....

3 Do whales and dolphins have rough skin or smooth skin?

.... **(1 mark)**

4 Humans have three kinds of teeth:

canines   molars   incisors

Fill in the gaps with the correct kind of teeth.

a. Teeth that are used for cutting are called .... **(1 mark)**

b. Teeth that are used for tearing are called .... **(1 mark)**

c. Teeth that are used for chewing are called

.... **(1 mark)**

5 How many teeth will you grow by the time you are an adult? **(1 mark)**

....

Total $\frac{}{20}$

The body and the senses

1 Tick (✓) the box next to the correct statement.   **(3 marks)**

   a. Braille is raised dots on paper that help blind people to read. ☐

      Braille is a layer of skin over the eyes. ☐

   b. The tiny dots on your tongue are called pimples. ☐

      The tiny dots on your tongue are called taste buds. ☐

   c. If you have a cold, your sense of smell gets better. ☐

      If you have a cold, you lose your sense of smell. ☐

2 Here is a picture of a child. Label the parts of the body.   **(18 marks)**

head   hair   face   nose   ear   eye   mouth   teeth   neck
shoulder   arm   hand   finger   thumb   leg   knee   foot   toe

Total —
21

Offspring

❶ Draw and label the life cycle of a butterfly. Put these stages in the right order. **(4 marks)**

pupa   egg   butterfly   caterpillar

❷ Draw lines to join the baby animals to their mothers. **(6 marks)**

calf	chicken
puppy	fox
lamb	cat
kitten	cow
chick	dog
cub	sheep

❸ What do baby mammals drink? .... **(1 mark)**

❹ How long is it before kittens' eyes open after they are born? **(1 mark)**

....

❺ What is a baby toad called? .... **(1 mark)**

❻ Put these words into the right order. **(5 marks)**

teenager   baby   child   adult   toddler

....

❼ What is a baby bird called when it is ready to fly from the nest? **(1 mark)**

....

Total $\frac{}{19}$

Survival

1 Which animals breathe through gills? .... **(1 mark)**

2 What is a blowhole? **(1 mark)**

....

....

3 Fill in the gaps. **(7 marks)**

lungs   gills   whales   mouth   porpoises   nose   dolphins

We breathe through our .... and ....

We breathe air into our ....

.... , ... and ....

breathe through a blowhole, but fish breathe through their

....

4 Tick (✔) the box next to the correct statement in each pair.   **(4 marks)**

a. Humans can last several weeks without water. ☐

Humans can only last a few days without water. ☐

b. There is water in fruit and vegetables. ☐

There is no water in fruit and vegetables. ☐

c. Contaminated water is good for you. ☐

Contaminated water can make you very ill. ☐

d. Smoke and fumes can harm your lungs. ☐

Smoke and fumes help you to be healthy. ☐

Total ⎯ 13

Food and hygiene

1 Circle the five foods that come from milk. **(5 marks)**

> yogurt   cake   carrots   butter   eggs   cream
>
> chips   cheese   nuts   bread   ice cream

2 Underline the six foods that come from plants. **(6 marks)**

> fish   lettuce   beans   chicken   potatoes
>
> soya milk   apple   prawns   banana

3 What might happen if you eat too much fatty food? **(1 mark)**

....

4 Draw and label **five fruits** and **five vegetables**. **(10 marks)**

5 How often should you exercise? .... **(1 mark)**

6 Name three ways you can exercise gently. **(3 marks)**

....

7 Name four ways you can exercise energetically. **(4 marks)**

....

8 Why is it important to clean your teeth twice a day? **(1 mark)**

....

Total — 31

Living, dead or never alive

❶ Fill in the gaps with the correct words.
Some words/phrases are used more than once. **(13 marks)**

> grow   breathe   seeds   touch and feel
> move about   alive   water   have babies   get rid of waste
> eat and drink   grow and change   alive

Animals, including humans, all do seven things:

- • ....
- • ....
- • ....
- • ....

- • ....
- • ....
- • ....

These actions tell us that they are ....

Plants do not ...., but they drink ....

from the soil, ... from a seed and make more

.... to grow into more plants. So they are

................................, too.

❷ Draw lines to sort each of these words/phrases into their correct set.
The first one has been done for you. **(12 marks)**

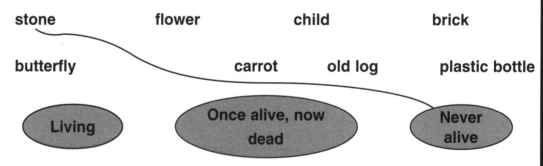

stone   flower   child   brick

butterfly   carrot   old log   plastic bottle

(Living)   (Once alive, now dead)   (Never alive)

wilted flower   tree

bucket   woodlouse on its back

Total — / 25

Basic needs of habitats

1 Complete each sentence.

a. A habitat is .... **(1 mark)**

....

b. Large fish and whales live in .... **(1 mark)**

....

c. Animals help plants by .... **(1 mark)**

....

d. Plants help animals by .... **(1 mark)**

....

2 Put a tick (✔) next to the statement if it is true and a cross (✗)
if it is false. **(6 marks)**

a. All animals live underground. ☐

b. Animals' habitats give them shelter from the
weather and danger. ☐

c. Some plants like to grow in the shade, some like
sunny places. ☐

d. Shellfish and crabs live in the middle of the deep ocean. ☐

e. Wild flowers grow where the habitat suits them best. ☐

f. Zoo animals live in their natural habitat. ☐

Total $\frac{}{10}$

Life inside habitats

1 Draw lines to join each animal with its habitat. **(6 marks)**

rabbit	sett
squirrel	nest
frog	den
fox	drey
badger	pond
blackbird	warren

2 Write each plant in the correct row to complete the table. **(7 marks)**

poppy   reeds   sunflower   bluebell

cactus   water lily   cow parsley

Plant	Habitat
....	shady woods
....	fields (in sunshine)
....	by a pond
....	by the roadside
....	hot, dry, sandy place
....	gardens
....	water

3 Which two things could you use to help you see tiny animals better? **(2 marks)**

....

Total ——
15

Food chains

❶ Circle six things that are at the bottom of their food chains. **(6 marks)**

rice   herbs   sheep   grass
frog   potato   flour   tiger   sugar   giraffe

❷ Tick (✓) the boxes next to the correct statements. **(3 marks)**

a. Nuts come from plants. ☐

b. Lions are at the top of their food chains. ☐

c. Humans are at the bottom of their food chains. ☐

d. Sparrows eat hawks. ☐

e. Herons eat frogs. ☐

f. Plants and smaller animals are at the top of their food chains. ☐

❸ Name three animals that milk comes from. **(3 marks)**

....

❹ Put these food chains in the right order. **(4 marks)**

a. deer   lion   grass

....

b. crocodile   weed   fish

....

c. bluetit   ant   owl

....

d. human   grass   sheep

....

Total $\frac{}{16}$

What objects are made of

❶ Write the name of each object and what it is made of. **(10 marks)**

....

....

....

....

❷ Fill in the gaps with the correct words.

| Windows | Jumpers | T-shirts | Bricks | Toilets |
| Pavements | Books | Shoes | | |

a. .... are made of concrete or tar. **(1 mark)**

b. .... are made of paper. **(1 mark)**

c. .... are made of glass. **(1 mark)**

d. .... are made of cotton. **(1 mark)**

e. .... are made of leather. **(1 mark)**

f. .... are made from clay. **(1 mark)**

g. .... are made from porcelain. **(1 mark)**

h. .... are made of wool. **(1 mark)**

Total — 18

Identifying and naming

1 Circle the six materials that are found in or under the ground. **(6 marks)**

diamond   wood   gold   oil   cotton

silver   leather   stone   rubber   emerald

2 Many objects are made of natural materials.

Tick (✓) the boxes next to the correct statements. **(4 marks)**

a. Cotton grows on plants so it is natural. ☐

b. Oil is made of melted-down plastic. ☐

c. Sand on the beach is made of millions of broken shells and rocks. ☐

d. A quarry is a deep hole where sand, stones and clay are dug out. ☐

e. Rubies are made of red glass. ☐

f. Water is a natural material that plants and animals need. ☐

3 What is glass made from? .... **(1 mark)**

4 What are bricks made from? .... **(1 mark)**

5 What is oil made from? **(1 mark)**

....

6 What is paper made from? **(1 mark)**

....

7 What are plates and dishes made of? .... **(1 mark)**

Total $\frac{}{15}$

Simple properties

❶ Draw lines to join these properties with their opposites. **(5 marks)**

rough	opaque
transparent	light
shiny	soft
hard	smooth
heavy	dull

❷ Choose two of these words to best describe each material. You can use each word more than once.

soft   smooth   light   bendy

thin   rough   waterproof   hard

a. wood   ....   **(2 marks)**

b. wool   ....   **(2 marks)**

c. plastic   ....   **(2 marks)**

d. paper   ....   **(2 marks)**

❸ Which two senses do you use to find out about properties of materials?   **(2 marks)**

....

....

Total $\frac{}{15}$

Grouping by properties

❶ Draw lines to sort these materials into three sets.
Some materials may be in more than one set. **(16 marks)**

diamond   wool   paper   plastic

fleece   metal   glass   fur

(Light)   (Soft)   (Shiny)

ruby   gold   silver   cotton

❷ Here are some objects made of materials.
Fill in the gaps to say whether they are **transparent** or **opaque**.

a. Brick walls are ....   **(1 mark)**

b. Car windscreens are ....   **(1 mark)**

c. Plastic bottles are usually ....   **(1 mark)**

d. Rocks and shells are ....   **(1 mark)**

e. Coins are ....   **(1 mark)**

f. A goldfish bowl is ....   **(1 mark)**

❸ **a.** Why do you need waterproof material to make
an umbrella?   **(1 mark)**

....

....

b. Name two materials that might be suitable
for making an umbrella.   **(2 marks)**

....

....

Total $\frac{}{25}$

Suitability for uses

1 Complete these sentences with one of the options below.

it is strong and keeps out the wind and weather.

it can be pressed into flat shapes that last for a very long time.

it is transparent and strong.

a. Metal is used for coins because… **(1 mark)**

....

....

b. Glass is used for windows because… **(1 mark)**

....

....

c. Wood is used for doors because… **(1 mark)**

....

....

2 When was the first plastic invented?

.... **(1 mark)**

3 Who invented waterproof material for coats? **(1 mark)**

....

4 From the list below, name two materials that each object can be made of.

wood   metal   plastic   brick   stone   glass

a. bottle	....	.... (2 marks)
b. fence	....	.... (2 marks)
c. spoon	....	.... (2 marks)
d. wall	....	.... (2 marks)

Total —
13

Changing shape

1 What happens to water when you boil it? **(1 mark)**

....

2 What happens to water when you freeze it? **(1 mark)**

....

3 What happens if ice is left out of the freezer?

.... **(1 mark)**

4 **a.** What happens when you heat chocolate? **(1 mark)**

....

b. Does the chocolate change back to how it was when it is cool?

.... **(1 mark)**

5 **a.** What happens when you burn paper? **(1 mark)**

....

b. Will it ever become paper again? .... **(1 mark)**

6 **a.** What happens to the different parts of an egg when you cook it?

the white: .... **(1 mark)**

the yolk: .... **(1 mark)**

b. Will the egg ever go back to how it was before cooking?

.... **(1 mark)**

7 **a.** What happens when you heat butter? **(1 mark)**

....

b. Will the butter be the same as it was when you cool it? **(2 marks)**

....

....

Total $\frac{}{13}$

1 Choose the healthier menu options by ticking (✓) one box
from each pair.   **(4 marks)**

Menu			
Boiled egg	☐	or Fried egg and bacon	☐
Sausage and mash	☐	or Ham salad	☐
Baked beans on toast	☐	or Burger and chips	☐
Chocolate pudding	☐	or Fruit salad	☐

2 Which sense do you use:

a. when you sniff a rose?   ....   **(1 mark)**

b. when you eat an apple?   ....   **(1 mark)**

c. when you listen to the radio?   ....   **(1 mark)**

d. when you pat a dog?   ....   **(1 mark)**

e. when you read a book?   ....   **(1 mark)**

3 Tick (✓) the boxes next to the correct statements.   **(3 marks)**

a. The ribs are bones that protect the heart and lungs.   ☐

b. Oil is a manufactured material.   ☐

c. The Sun is at its highest in winter.   ☐

d. If you heat butter it changes to a liquid.   ☐

e. Windows are opaque.   ☐

f. Snakes and crocodiles are reptiles.   ☐

4 Where does an emerald come from?   ....   **(1 mark)**

5 What is a badger's habitat called?   ....   **(1 mark)**

6 What is a baby sheep called?   ....   **(1 mark)**

7 Is leather a natural material? .... **(1 mark)**

8 Name two evergreen trees. **(2 marks)**

....

9 What is a drought? **(1 mark)**

....

10 Which animal lives in a warren? .... **(1 mark)**

11 Fill in the gaps. **(2 marks)**
The Sun gives us .... and ....

12 What are vertebrae? **(1 mark)**

....

13 What is a micro-habitat? **(1 mark)**

....

....

14 What happens to a plant if it has no water? .... **(1 mark)**

15 Answer these questions.

a. How many legs does a spider have? .... **(1 mark)**

b. What is another word for the spine? .... **(1 mark)**

c. How many limbs do humans have? .... **(1 mark)**

d. Why do cows have strong molar teeth? .... **(1 mark)**

e. Do evergreen trees lose their leaves in autumn? .... **(1 mark)**

f. What are clouds made of? .... **(1 mark)**

g. Name one way that plants help animals. **(1 mark)**

....

h. Is a rotting log living, dead, or
once alive but now dead? .... **(1 mark)**

i. Why do we need to exercise? .... **(1 mark)**

j. What is a predator? .... **(1 mark)**

16 Complete the table by writing the correct type of body covering in each row. **(10 marks)**

hard shell   smooth skin   fur   scaly skin   feathers

Animal	Body covering
snake	
tortoise	
eagle	
bear	
dolphin	
frog	
cat	
beetle	
bird	
fish	

17 Fill in the gaps with the correct words.

bulb   joints   cub   gills   recycled
skin   plants   skeleton   metal   milk

a. Elbows, knees, wrists and ankles are all .... **(1 mark)**

b. A fork is made of .... **(1 mark)**

c. Things that are used again instead of being thrown away

are .... **(1 mark)**

d. A baby fox is called a .... **(1 mark)**

e. Female dolphins feed their young on .... **(1 mark)**

f. As snakes grow they shed their .... **(1 mark)**

g. The frame of bones that supports the body of an animal

is a .... **(1 mark)**

h. A daffodil grows from a .... **(1 mark)**

i. Fish breathe through their .... **(1 mark)**

j. Rice, sugar and flour come from .... **(1 mark)**

18 Draw and label the life cycle of the frog.   **(3 marks)**

19 Fill in the gaps with the correct words.   **(11 marks)**

crystal   sleet   plants   rain   six
water droplets   winter   snow   hail   water   clouds

.... and animals need .... to survive. Water

falls as ...., which comes from .... Clouds

are made of ....

In ...., there might be a few snowflakes in the rain. This is

called .... On other days, the rain falls as small pieces of ice.

This is called ....

.... is water that is frozen into beautiful ice crystals. Each

.... is like a .... pointed star.

20 Draw lines to sort these materials into two sets.   **(14 marks)**

wool   **glass**   **plastic**   **water**

oil   **brick**   **stone**   **wood**   **china**

paper   (**Natural**)   (**Manufactured**)   **cotton**

sand   **concrete**   **clay**

PLANTS

Test Yourself Questions

page 5
1 cedar (oak) (beech) pine
2 cultivated
3 because it contains seeds
4 buttercup, violet, dandelion
   (**accept other appropriate answers**)

page 7
1 **Accept any three from:** daffodil, hyacinth, tulip, crocus (**or other appropriate answers**)
2 the fruit
3 dandelion seed head
4 to protect the trunk and branches

page 9
1 acorn
2 water, light and warmth
3 through the roots and up the stem
4 asleep; ready to be active when the time is right

Practice Questions

page 11
1 a. acorn **(1 mark)**   d. conker **(1 mark)**
   b. pip **(1 mark)**   e. seed in a stone
   c. pine nut **(1 mark)**   **(1 mark)**
2 stem   **(1 mark)**
3 holly   **(1 mark)**
4 blossom   **(1 mark)**
5 onion, garlic, leek   **(3 marks)**
6 roots   **(1 mark)**
7

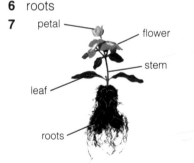

petal — flower
stem
leaf
roots

   (5 marks: award 1 mark for each correct answer)

SEASONAL CHANGES

Test Yourself Questions

page 13
1 spring, summer, autumn, winter
2 winter
3 autumn
4 winter

page 15
1 six
2 **Accept any four from:** drink, wash hands, have baths, have showers, wash clothes, farming, water garden
3 water droplets
4 light and warmth

Practice Questions

page 17
1 a. spring **(1 mark)**   d. spring **(1 mark)**
   b. winter **(1 mark)**   e. winter **(1 mark)**
   c. summer **(1 mark)**   f. autumn **(1 mark)**
2 (frog) cat mouse (hedgehog)
   robin (toad) rabbit   **(3 marks)**
3 There is less food; to shelter from the cold.
                (2 marks: award 1 mark for each correct answer)
4 It is colder and we need to keep warm.
   (2 marks: award 1 mark for each correct answer)
5 to lay eggs (frogspawn)   **(1 mark)**
6 snowdrop   **(1 mark)**
7 It could damage your eyes. **(1 mark)**
8 Drought is when there has been no rain for a long time. ✓ **(1 mark)**

ANIMALS, INCLUDING HUMANS

Test Yourself Questions

page 19
1 tortoise
2 blue whale
3 (whale) (mouse) haddock (cow)
   newt ostrich (gerbil) salmon (fox)

page 21
1 hunting
2 lion **sheep** **elephant** cat **panda** bear rat **beaver** tiger
3 plants and animals

page 23
1 spine
2 tortoise, crab, beetle
   (**accept other appropriate answers**)
3 scaly

page 25
1 five: hearing, sight, touch, taste, smell
2 taste buds
3 to protect eyes and keep them clean and moist
4 dog/guide dog

page 27

1 a tiny egg inside (a blob of) jelly
2 calf
3 guinea pig
4 **Accept any two from:** whale, porpoise, dolphin

page 29

1 air, water, food
2 fish
3 **Accept one from:** smoke, traffic fumes **(or other appropriate answers)**

page 31

1 put on weight; damage teeth
2 fatty food
3 wash hands, bath or shower, clean teeth regularly

Practice Questions

page 33

1 **a.** animal that eats meat/other animals
   (1 mark)
   b. animal that eats no meat/only plants
   (1 mark)
2 **a.** arms, legs, wings **(3 marks)**
   b. <u>snake</u>, <u>shark</u>, <u>dolphin</u> **(3 marks)**
3 octopus, spider **(2 marks)**
4
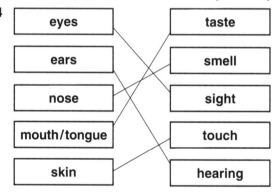

(5 marks: award 1 mark for each correct match)

5 When a caterpillar makes a shell around itself; it emerges later as a butterfly or moth.
   (1 mark)
6 air, water, food **(3 marks)**
7 fish   nuts   (cakes)   milk   (fizzy drinks)
   carrots   (chocolate) **(3 marks)**
8 apples   <u>chips</u>   <u>pizza</u>   egg
   dried apricots   <u>crisps</u>   cabbage **(3 marks)**

LIVING THINGS AND THEIR HABITATS

Test Yourself Questions

page 35

1 eat and drink; move about; breathe; touch and feel; grow and change; get rid of waste (go to the toilet); have babies

2 It does not do any of the things listed in question 1.
3 (dog)   money   fence   (human)
   (tree)   shoe   chimney   (baby)   (rose)

page 37

1 the weather and danger
2 grow more plants or animals; for example, from seeds or eggs
3 (underground)   inside a car
   (a rainforest)   (up a tree)   (in the ocean)
4 **Accept:** crabs, shellfish, seabirds **(or other appropriate answers)**

page 39

1 shelter, warmth, comfort, favourite things, food and drink
2 earth
3 squirrel
4 **Accept one from:** primrose, bluebell, wood anemone **(or other appropriate answers)**

page 41

1 dandelion, rabbit, fox
2 mouse   <u>human</u>   <u>eagle</u>   worm
   <u>tiger</u>   rabbit   <u>lion</u>   <u>killer whale</u>
3 eggs   (potatoes)   (rice)   milk
   (nuts)   (sugar)   cheese   (flour)

Practice Questions

page 43

1 bone   <u>flower</u>   car   <u>cat</u>   <u>holly tree</u>
   shell   table   <u>hedgehog</u>   pencil **(4 marks)**
2 Rocks have never been alive. ✓
   A shell was once alive, now dead. ✓
   (2 marks: award 1 mark for each correct answer)
3 the natural home or environment of an animal, plant, or other living thing **(1 mark)**
4 **Accept one from:** water lily, forget-me-not, reeds, iris **(1 mark)**
5 **Accept one from:** cactus, tumbleweed, palm tree **(1 mark)**
6 squirrel   (rabbit)   hedgehog   horse
   (badger)   frog **(2 marks)**
7 to study tiny things more closely **(1 mark)**
8 **Accept four from:** milk, cheese, butter, yogurt, cream, ice cream **(4 marks)**
9 fly ⟶ frog ⟶ heron **(1 mark)**
10 seeds, grass
   (or other appropriate answers)
   (2 marks: award 1 mark for each correct answer)

EVERYDAY MATERIALS

Test Yourself Questions

page 45

1 a thing

2 what objects are made of

3 metal or plastic

4 <u>chair</u> toilet <u>fence</u> chimney <u>table</u> <u>door</u> coat <u>cupboard</u>

page 47

1 wood (stone) (clay) plastic wool (silver) leather (rubies)

2 plastic <u>wool</u> <u>oil</u> glass <u>sand</u> <u>wood</u> paper <u>diamond</u>

3 a cotton plant

page 49

1 sight and touch

2 Wood is strong and hard. ✓

3 **a.** dull **b.** light **c.** smooth

Page 51

1 hard, shiny, transparent

2 feather, paper, cotton wool

3 hard, heavy, rough
(**or other appropriate answers**)

4 glass, plastic, metal
(**or other appropriate answers**)

page 53

1 (brick) feathers (stone) (concrete) cotton (glass) shells

2 They know the properties of the materials.

3 **Any three from:** plastic, wood, metal, clay, porcelain

4 <u>coin</u> window raincoat <u>saucepan</u> <u>gate</u> toothbrush <u>screw</u> <u>door handle</u>

page 55

1 It turns into a powder called ash.

2 chocolate, plastic, glass
(**or other appropriate answers**)

3 paper folding to make different shapes

4 water and sand

page 57

1 It turns from a liquid to a solid and from transparent to opaque.

2 It becomes solid.

3 No – it goes solid but has a different texture.

Practice Questions

page 59

1

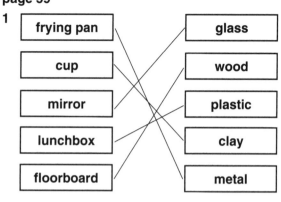

(**5 marks: award 1 mark for each correct match**)

2 **a.** They are dug out of the ground. (**1 mark**)
  b. animal skin (**1 mark**)

3 **a.** wood, recycled paper, old clothes (**3 marks**)
  b. clay (**1 mark**)

4 hard, shiny, transparent (**3 marks**)

5 **a.** paper (**1 mark**)
  b. glass (**1 mark**)

6 **a.** it becomes liquid (**1 mark**)
  b. it turns to ash (**1 mark**)

WORKBOOK

PLANTS

page 60

1 They might become extinct (none left).
(**1 mark**)

2 **a.** dandelion **w** (**1 mark**)
  b. pansy **c** (**1 mark**)
  c. sweet pea **c** (**1 mark**)
  d. clover **w** (**1 mark**)

3 The fruit and vegetables are ready for harvesting and eating. (**1 mark**)

4 banana (courgette) orange (pepper) (cucumber) blackcurrant (**3 marks**)

5 (raspberry) potato (pear) lettuce carrot (strawberry) parsnip (**3 marks**)

6 Different kinds of trees have different-shaped **leaves**. Deciduous trees lose their leaves in **autumn**. Evergreen trees have leaves all **year** round. Some evergreen trees have **needles** and some have **dark** green **shiny** leaves. (**6 marks**)

page 61

1 autumn (**1 mark**)

2 spring (**1 mark**)

3 **a.** Lettuce, cabbage and spinach are the **leaf** of the plant. (**1 mark**)
  b. Cauliflower and broccoli are the **flower** of a plant. (**1 mark**)

c. Carrots and parsnips are the
root of a plant. **(1 mark)**

4 branch   leaf   **(5 marks)**

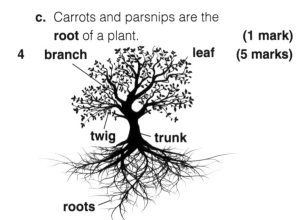

twig   trunk

roots

page 62

1 onion, garlic, leek   **(3 marks)**
(**or other appropriate answers**)

2 **a.** deciduous   **(1 mark)**
   b. evergreen   **(1 mark)**
   c. evergreen   **(1 mark)**
   d. deciduous   **(1 mark)**

3 It will wilt and die.   **(1 mark)**

4 underground; stored in a dry place
      (2 marks: award 1 mark for each point)

5 conker   **(1 mark)**

6 pine nut   **(1 mark)**

7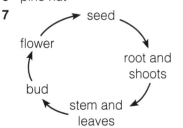
seed
flower
root and shoots
bud
stem and leaves

**(5 marks: award 1 mark for each label that
is in the correct place)**

SEASONAL CHANGES

page 63

1 summer   **(1 mark)**
2 summer   **(1 mark)**
3 autumn   **(1 mark)**
4 summer   **(1 mark)**
5 a deep sleep which some animals
fall into during winter   **(1 mark)**
6 when birds fly long distances from
one country to another, according
to the seasons   **(1 mark)**
7 spring   **(1 mark)**
8 spring   **(1 mark)**
9 Picture of a tree during each of the four
seasons: spring with buds and beginning
of leaves **(1 mark)**; summer in full leaf
(1 mark); autumn with orange and gold
leaves, with some on the ground **(1 mark)**;
winter with bare branches **(1 mark)**

page 64

1 **a.** Water droplets fall as **rain** in
warm weather.   **(1 mark)**
   b. **Hail** is pieces of frozen rain.   **(1 mark)**
   c. When rain contains some ice
or snowflakes, it is called **sleet**.   **(1 mark)**
   d. The word **snow** describes tiny ice
crystals that fall as white flakes.   **(1 mark)**

2 **a.** A reservoir is a large lake
where water is stored.   ✓   **(1 mark)**
   b. A hurricane is a strong wind
that causes damage.   ✓   **(1 mark)**
   c. A rainbow appears when
the Sun shines and it rains.   ✓   **(1 mark)**

3 Plants need rain to help them **grow**.
Animals and birds need rain to **drink**.
Humans need water for drinking, washing
hands, bathing, washing clothes and
watering the garden.
If there is too much rain there might be
floods. If there is no rain for a long time,
there will be a **drought**.   **(7 marks)**

ANIMALS, INCLUDING HUMANS

page 65

1 **Accept five labelled drawings**. Examples
of pets could be hamster, guinea pig, gerbil,
cat, dog, rabbit, horse, mouse, rat.
**(5 marks: award 1 mark for each
completed drawing with label)**

2 frog, toad, newt   **(3 marks)**

3 **a.** A mole is a **mammal**.   **(1 mark)**
   b. A dolphin is a **mammal**.   **(1 mark)**
   c. A toad is an **amphibian**.   **(1 mark)**
   d. An eagle is a **bird**.   **(1 mark)**
   e. A snake is a **reptile**.   **(1 mark)**
   f. A bear is a **mammal**.   **(1 mark)**
   g. A butterfly is an **insect**.   **(1 mark)**
   h. A shark is a **fish**.   **(1 mark)**
   i. An ostrich is a **bird**.   **(1 mark)**
   j. A turtle is a **reptile**.   **(1 mark)**

page 66

1 tiny sea creatures called plankton   **(1 mark)**
2 **Accept two from:** other whales, dolphins,
seals, fish   **(2 marks)**
3 orca   **(1 mark)**
4 **Accept one from:** killer whales have sharp
teeth, baleen whale don't; baleen whales are
usually larger; baleen whales tend to swim
alone, killer whales swim in groups
      (1 mark)
5 smaller birds and animals   **(1 mark)**
6 It eats other animals but also berries,
nuts and fruit.   **(1 mark)**

7 vegetarians (1 mark)

8 a. A tiger is **a carnivore**. (1 mark)
  b. A panda is **a herbivore**. (1 mark)
  c. A tadpole is **a herbivore**. (1 mark)
  d. A frog is **a carnivore**. (1 mark)
  e. A crocodile is **a carnivore**. (1 mark)
  f. A bear is **an omnivore**. (1 mark)
  g. A rabbit is **a herbivore**. (1 mark)

page 67

1
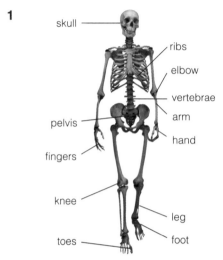

skull
ribs
elbow
vertebrae
pelvis
arm
hand
fingers
knee
leg
toes
foot

(12 marks: award 1 mark for each correctly labelled part)

2 arms, legs, wings **(3 marks)**
3 smooth skin **(1 mark)**
4 a. incisors **(1 mark)**
  b. canines **(1 mark)**
  c. molars **(1 mark)**
5 32 **(1 mark)**

page 68

1 a. Braille is raised dots on paper that help blind people to read. ✓ **(1 mark)**
  b. The tiny dots on your tongue are called taste buds. ✓ **(1 mark)**
  c. If you have a cold, you lose your sense of smell. ✓ **(1 mark)**

2
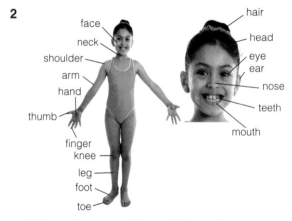

face
neck
shoulder
arm
hand
thumb
finger
knee
leg
foot
toe
hair
head
eye
ear
nose
teeth
mouth

(18 marks: award 1 mark for each correctly labelled part)

page 69

1
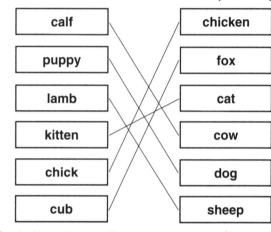

egg
caterpillar
butterfly
pupa

(4 marks: award 1 mark for each label that is in the correct place)

2 **(6 marks)**

calf	chicken
puppy	fox
lamb	cat
kitten	cow
chick	dog
cub	sheep

3 their mother's milk **(1 mark)**
4 one or two weeks **(1 mark)**
5 a tadpole **(1 mark)**
6 baby, toddler, child, teenager, adult **(5 marks)**
7 a fledgling **(1 mark)**

page 70

1 fish **(1 mark)**
2 A hole in the top of the head of whales, dolphins and porpoises which acts as their nostril. **(1 mark)**
3 We breathe through our **mouth** and **nose**. We breathe air into our **lungs**. **Whales**, **dolphins** and **porpoises** [list in any order] breathe through a blowhole, but fish breathe through their **gills**. **(7 marks)**
4 a. Humans can only last a few days without water. ✓ **(1 mark)**
  b. There is water in fruit and vegetables. ✓ **(1 mark)**
  c. Contaminated water can make you very ill. ✓ **(1 mark)**
  d. Smoke and fumes can harm your lungs. ✓ **(1 mark)**

page 71

1 (yogurt) cake carrots (butter) eggs (cream) chips (cheese) nuts bread (ice cream) **(5 marks)**
2 fish lettuce beans chicken potatoes soya milk apple prawns banana **(6 marks)**
3 You might put on weight. **(1 mark)**

4 **Accept five labelled fruit drawings and five labelled vegetable drawings.**
Examples of fruit: apple, pear, peach, orange, banana, apricot, strawberry, raspberry, kiwi, pineapple. **(5 marks)**
Examples of vegetables: broccoli, cabbage, leek, onion, beans, carrot, parsnip. **(5 marks)**

5 every day **(1 mark)**

6 walking to school, walking in the countryside, playing in the playground (**accept other appropriate answers**) **(3 marks)**

7 swimming, gymnastics, football, cycling fast, climbing trees (**accept other appropriate answers**) **(4 marks)**

8 to prevent tooth decay **(1 mark)**

LIVING THINGS AND THEIR HABITATS

page 72

1 Animals, including humans all do seven things:
- **breathe**
- **grow and change**
- **touch and feel**
- **move about**
- **have babies**
- **get rid of waste**
- **eat and drink**

These actions tell us that they are **alive**. Plants do not **move about**, but they drink **water** from the soil, **grow** from a seed and make more **seeds** to grow into more plants. So they are **alive**, too. **(12 marks)**

2 **Living**: flower, child, butterfly, carrot, tree **(5 marks)**

Once alive, now dead: old log, wilted flower, woodlouse on its back **(3 marks)**
Never alive: stone, brick, plastic bottle, bucket **(4 marks)**

page 73

1 **a.** A habitat is **the natural home of a living thing**. **(1 mark)**
b. Large fish and whales live in **the ocean**. **(1 mark)**
c. Animals help plants by **carrying seeds from one place to another**. **(1 mark)**
d. Plants help animals by **giving them food and shelter**. **(1 mark)**

2 **a.** All animals live underground. ✗
b. Animals' habitats give them shelter from the weather and danger. ✓
c. Some plants like to grow in the shade, some like sunny places. ✓

d. Shellfish and crabs live in the middle of the deep ocean. ✗
e. Wild flowers grow where the habitat suits them best. ✓
f. Zoo animals live in their natural habitat. ✗
(6 marks)

page 74

1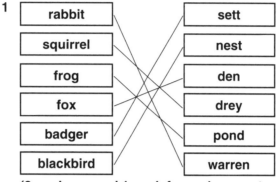
(**6 marks: award 1 mark for each correct match**)

2

Plant	Habitat
bluebell	shady woods
poppy	fields (in sunshine)
reeds	by a pond
cow parsley	by the roadside
cactus	hot, dry, sandy place
sunflower	gardens
water lily	water

(7 marks)

3 microscope; magnifying glass **(2 marks)**

page 75

1 (rice) (herbs) sheep (grass) frog (potato) (flour) tiger (sugar) giraffe **(6 marks)**

2 **a.** Nuts come from plants. ✓ **(1 mark)**
b. Lions are at the top of their food chains. ✓ **(1 mark)**
e. Herons eat frogs. ✓ **(1 mark)**

3 cow, sheep, goat **(3 marks)**

4 **a.** grass, deer, lion **(1 mark)**
b. weed, fish, crocodile **(1 mark)**
c. ant, bluetit, owl **(1 mark)**
d. grass, sheep, human **(1 mark)**

EVERYDAY MATERIALS

page 76

1 jug: glass **(2 marks)**; chair: wood **(2 marks)**; toy / blocks: plastic **(2 marks)**; saucepan: metal **(2 marks)**; cup and saucer: pottery / clay **(2 marks)**

2
a. **Pavements** are made of concrete or tar. **(1 mark)**
b. **Books** are made of paper. **(1 mark)**
c. **Windows** are made of glass. **(1 mark)**
d. **T-shirts** are made of cotton. **(1 mark)**
e. **Shoes** are made of leather. **(1 mark)**
f. **Bricks** are made from clay. **(1 mark)**
g. **Toilets** are made from porcelain. **(1 mark)**
h. **Jumpers** are made of wool. **(1 mark)**

page 77

1 (diamond) wood (gold) (oil) cotton
(silver) leather (stone) rubber (emerald)
(6 marks)

2
a. Cotton grows on plants so it is natural. ✓ **(1 mark)**
c. Sand on the beach is made of millions of broken shells and rocks. ✓ **(1 mark)**
d. A quarry is a deep hole where sand, stones and clay are dug out. ✓ **(1 mark)**
f. Water is a natural material that plants and animals need. ✓ **(1 mark)**

3 sand **(1 mark)**
4 clay **(1 mark)**
5 millions of tiny creatures that lived millions of years ago **(1 mark)**
6 wood or recycled paper or old clothes **(1 mark)**
7 clay **(1 mark)**

page 78

1

rough	opaque
transparent	light
shiny	soft
hard	smooth
heavy	dull

(5 marks)

2
a. wood **accept two from: hard, rough, bendy, light** **(2 marks)**
b. wool **soft, light** **(2 marks)**
c. plastic **smooth, waterproof** **(2 marks)**
d. paper **light, thin** **(2 marks)**

3 sight, touch **(2 marks)**

page 79

1 **Light**: paper, wool, plastic, fleece, fur **(5 marks)**
Soft: fleece, wool, fur, cotton **(4 marks)**
Shiny: diamond, glass, plastic, metal, ruby, gold, silver **(7 marks)**

2
a. Brick walls are **opaque**. **(1 mark)**
b. Car windscreens are **transparent**. **(1 mark)**
c. Plastic bottles are usually **transparent**. **(1 mark)**
d. Rocks and shells are **opaque**. **(1 mark)**
e. Coins are **opaque**. **(1 mark)**
f. A goldfish bowl is **transparent**. **(1 mark)**

3
a. to protect you from the rain (an absorbent material would let rain through) **(1 mark)**
b. **Accept two from:** polythene, aluminium foil, plastic **(2 marks)**

page 80

1
a. Metal is used for coins because **it can be pressed into flat shapes that last for a very long time**. **(1 mark)**
b. Glass is used for windows because **it is transparent and strong**. **(1 mark)**
c. Wood is used for doors because **it is strong and keeps out the wind and weather**. **(1 mark)**

2 nineteenth century **(1 mark)**
3 Charles Macintosh **(1 mark)**
4
a. bottle **glass plastic** **(2 marks)**
b. fence **wood metal/plastic** **(2 marks)**
c. spoon **plastic metal/wood** **(2 marks)**
d. wall **brick stone** **(2 marks)**

page 81

1 It changes to steam (gas). **(1 mark)**
2 It changes to ice (solid). **(1 mark)**
3 It melts. **(1 mark)**
4
a. It goes soft, then runny (liquid). **(1 mark)**
b. yes **(1 mark)**
5
a. It turns to ash. **(1 mark)**
b. no **(1 mark)**
6
a. the white: changes from transparent to opaque and liquid to solid **(1 mark)**
the yolk: becomes solid if you cook it for more than five minutes **(1 mark)**
b. no **(1 mark)**
7
a. It melts into a transparent liquid. **(1 mark)**
b. Yes and no – it becomes solid when cooled, but it is not the same as before it was heated. **(2 marks)**

Mixed Practice Questions
pages 82–85

1 Boiled egg ✓ (1 mark)
   Ham salad ✓ (1 mark)
   Baked beans on toast ✓ (1 mark)
   Fruit salad ✓ (1 mark)

2 **a.** when you sniff a rose? **smell** (1 mark)
   b. when you eat an apple? **taste** (1 mark)
   c. when you listen to the radio? **hearing** (1 mark)
   d. when you pat a dog? **touch** (1 mark)
   e. when you read a book? **sight** (1 mark)

3 **a.** The ribs are bones that protect the heart and lungs. ✓ (1 mark)
   d. If you heat butter it changes to a liquid. ✓ (1 mark)
   f. Snakes and crocodiles are reptiles. ✓ (1 mark)

4 under the ground (1 mark)
5 sett (1 mark)
6 lamb (1 mark)
7 yes (1 mark)
8 **Accept any two from:** holly, pine, fir, larch, cedar (2 marks)
9 when there is little or no rain for a long time (1 mark)
10 rabbit (1 mark)
11 The Sun gives us **light** and **warmth**. (2 marks)
12 the long line of bones that make up the backbone (1 mark)
13 a miniature habitat where the environment is different from the surrounding area (1 mark)
14 It wilts and dies. (1 mark)
15 **a.** eight (1 mark)
   b. backbone (1 mark)
   c. four (two arms; two legs) (1 mark)
   d. so they can chew grass (1 mark)
   e. no (1 mark)
   f. water droplets (1 mark)
   g. by giving them food/shelter (1 mark)
   h. once alive but now dead (1 mark)
   i. to strengthen our bones and muscles, and to keep us healthy (1 mark)
   j. an animal that hunts and kills other animals for food (1 mark)

16.

Animal	Body covering
snake	**scaly skin**
tortoise	**hard shell**
eagle	**feathers**
bear	**fur**
dolphin	**smooth skin**
frog	**smooth skin**
cat	**fur**
beetle	**hard shell**
bird	**feathers**
fish	**scaly skin**

(10 marks)

17 **a.** Elbows, knees, wrists and ankles are all **joints**. (1 mark)
   b. A fork is made of **metal**. (1 mark)
   c. Things that are used again instead of being thrown away are **recycled**. (1 mark)
   d. A baby fox is called a **cub**. (1 mark)
   e. Female dolphins feed their young on **milk**. (1 mark)
   f. As snakes grow they shed their **skin**. (1 mark)
   g. The frame of bones that supports the body of an animal is a **skeleton**. (1 mark)
   h. A daffodil grows from a **bulb**. (1 mark)
   i. Fish breathe through their **gills**. (1 mark)
   j. Rice, sugar and flour come from **plants**. (1 mark)

18 (3 marks)

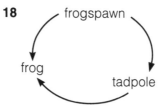

19 **Plants** and animals need **water** to survive. Water falls as **rain**, which comes from **clouds**. Clouds are made of **water droplets**. In **winter**, there might be a few snowflakes in the rain. This is called **sleet**. On other days, the rain falls as small pieces of ice. This is called **hail**. **Snow** is water that is frozen into beautiful ice crystals. Each **crystal** is like a **six**-pointed star. (11 marks)

20 **Natural**: wool, water, oil, stone, wood, cotton, sand, clay (8 marks)
   Manufactured: glass, plastic, brick, china, paper, concrete (6 marks)

Absorbent – It will soak up liquid

Ash – A grey or white powder that forms after materials like wood and paper are burned

Bark – The protective skin of trees and shrubs

Blowhole – A hole in the top of the head of whales, dolphins and porpoises, which acts as their nostril

Braille – The alphabet as a series of patterned dots raised on a page

Breed – To grow more plants or animals, e.g. from seeds or eggs

Bulb – Bulbs are usually round. The shoot is in the centre of the bulb. Inside the bulb's outer skin there are many fleshy layers that contain food for the shoot

Contaminated – Unclean, polluted or poisoned

Cultivated – Plants that are grown and cared for

Deciduous – A tree or plant that sheds its leaves in autumn every year

Dissolve – Dissolving is when you mix something with a liquid until it seems to become part of the liquid

Dormant – Asleep and ready to be active when the time is right

Drought – When there is no rain for a long time. The ground dries, plants die, and animals and humans do not have enough water

Energy – The power to do things; what keeps us active and alert

Evergreen – A tree that has leaves all year round

Flood – When there is too much water in a short time. River banks burst and water runs over the land and sometimes floods buildings

Fossil – The remains of animals and plants that died a long time ago

Frogspawn – A tiny egg inside a blob of jelly

Gills – On the sides of a fish's head. The fish breathes through them

Habitat – The natural home or environment of an animal, plant or other living thing

Hibernate – A deep sleep which some animals fall into during winter

Hurricane – A very, very strong wind that blows down trees and damages buildings

Limbs – Arms or legs of a human or animal, or birds' wings

Liquid – Flows freely

Lungs – Two spongy sacks inside the chest

Manufactured – Made by people who change a natural material to make it into something completely different, usually in combination with other things

Manufacturers – People who make things for us to buy; this is often done in a factory

Mammals – Warm-blooded animals that give birth to babies and feed them with milk

Material – What objects are made of

Micro-habitat – A miniature habitat within a larger one; an area where the environment is different from the world around it

Migrate – Birds fly long distances from one country to another, according to the seasons

Muscles – Joined to bones and help the bones move

Natural – Materials that come from nature; they are not made by humans

Object A thing

Opaque – Not see-through

Predator – A wild animal that hunts other animals for food

Properties – What a material is like; for example, hard, soft

Protein – Helps our bodies to grow and our muscles to become strong

Pupa – An insect at the stage between caterpillar and adult, when it has a hard covering

Quarry – A deep hole where stones and sand are dug out of the ground

Raptor – A bird that hunts for its food. It has a hooked bill and sharp talons. It is also called a bird of prey

Recycled – When the material an object is made from is used again

Reservoir – A lake specially made for storing water

Ribs – Like a cage of bones to protect your heart and lungs

Ripe – Fruit and vegetables that are fully developed and ready for harvesting and eating

Seed – A small object produced by a plant from which a new plant can grow

Set – Another word for group

Sight – The ability to see

Skeleton – A framework of bones inside the body that supports the body of an animal

Skull – The hard bone of your head that protects your brain

Solid – A material that is firm and hard

Steam – A gas, a white mist of water droplets in the air, which is formed when water is boiled

Texture – What the surface of an object feels like

Transparent – See-through

Vegetarian – A person who does not eat meat or fish

Vertebrae – Small bones that form the backbone

Vitamins – Help us to make the best use of our food and to fight diseases

Vivarium – A container to keep animals in

Wild – Plants that grow naturally without human help

Wilt – Become limp and droop, often turning yellow and then brown